SOP

CW00818978

NOVELLO EWER & C? LITHO,

THE ART OF

SWIMMING

BY

CAPTAIN WEBB,

THE CHANNEL SWIMMER.

(EDITED BY A. G. PAYNE.)

PRYOR PUBLICATIONS

WHITSTABLE AND WALSALL

PRYOR PUBLICATIONS
WHITSTABLE AND WALSALL

Specialist in Facsimile Reproductions.

MEMBER OF
INDEPENDENT PUBLISHERS GUILD

75 Dargate Road, Yorkletts, Whitstable,
Kent CT5 3AE, England.
Tel. & Fax: (01227) 274655
Email: alan@pryor-publish.clara.net
www.pryor-publish.clara.net

Kent Exporter of the Year Awards Winner 1998

© Pryor Publications 1999

ISBN 0 946014 78 7

A full list of Titles sent free on request

First published around 1876

WARD, LOCK AND TYLER,
WARWICK HOUSE, PATERNOSTER ROW.

Cover Reconstruction
by Simon Scamp

Printed and bound in Great Britain by
MPG Books Ltd, Bodmin, Cornwall

CONTENTS.

This Book is Dedicated to
Robin

MY LIFE.

I WAS born at Dawley, Shropshire, on the 19th January, 1848. My father was a medical man (whose practice was more extensive than lucrative) and I am one of twelve children. It would be, perhaps, difficult for me to say exactly what is my earliest recollection. Strange to say, however, it is connected with the water; but whether it was a pond, or the River Severn, which ran near our house, in which I learned to swim when I was eight years of age, I cannot say positively.

I do not wish to boast, but, as I am writing what I believe will be essentially a book for boys, I will run the risk of being laughed at for blowing my own trumpet, in order that what I say may be of service to others. As a child I had an instinctive horror of a lie. So much was this feeling embedded in my child-mind, that I was peculiarly sensitive to anything appearing like a want of truthfulness in others; and there are two little anecdotes told of me by my mother, neither of which, however, do I recollect, that happened when I was very young indeed. I used to wonder why it was that my father used to go out regularly every morning so early. My mother told me, "that it was to get the bread and cheese." A few mornings afterwards, on seeing my father pack up some bread and cheese for luncheon to carry with him, I am reported to have indignantly exclaimed: "There, mamma, you said papa went out to get the bread and cheese, and he takes it with him." Another somewhat similar instance of my sensitiveness on this point of truthfulness occurred when I was looking over some pictures. It was an old engraving, familiar to most children, of Daniel in the Lion's Den, and the lions were drawn, as they usually are, roaring with their mouths open; while Daniel, with his hands folded, looked calmly on. I had been religiously brought up, and when I saw the picture, I said to my mother: "That is not true then, what you told me, mamma, as you said God shut the lions' mouths, and you see they have got them all wide open."

One of my earliest recollections is lying in my little bed at night, and building what are known as "castles in the air." From a very early period of my life I had a longing for the sea—a longing that was partially fostered by some story-books telling of the perils and adventures of the deep. Often, when I have been lying awake at night, have I pictured to my mind what a storm at sea would be like. Sometimes on windy evenings, when the clouds were chasing each other across

the moon, have I crept out of my little bed to the
window, and watched the elms tossing their giant
arms aloft in the air, and as the wind moaned
through them, I fancied that I heard it whistling
through the rigging. I have since been in many
a storm at sea, and I must honestly confess that my
youthful imagination pictured a far different scene to
the reality.

As I said before, I learnt to swim at a very
early age. I have no doubt some older boy can
claim the credit of having taught me or shown
me, but I have no recollection of his name.
I used, in company with other boys, during the
summer-months, to go down to the River Severn,
and paddle about. Being a tolerably healthy child,
at eight I was a very fairly good swimmer. Little
did I think at the time that what I was then
learning would turn out to be more useful to me
than anything else that I have ever learnt in my life.
As I have before hinted, I was an imaginative child;
and often have I dreamed or pictured to myself, in
day-dreams, of performing some great feat or act
of heroism. I have imagined myself commanding
a ship, and of being successful in some great naval
engagement. Sometimes I have thought of performing the feat of rescuing some lovely creature from
some great peril; but I must honestly say, that on
this point, considering how young I was, my thoughts
were very vague. It certainly never did occur to me

that the great feat that I should perform, and one
that would make me a name in after-life, would be
a feat of swimming. I suppose it will always be
found that what we dream and imagine most when
we are young rarely turns out to be true in
mature age.

One very strong feeling with me, however, was
my determination not to be a burden to my parents.
As I have said, my father's health was far from
good, and his practice was, in consequence,
not particularly large. Having so many brothers
and sisters, some older and some younger than
myself, I determined, if possible, to make my own
living; in what I did not care, so long as I should
not be a burden to them. And it was at my own
request that, at the age of twelve, I joined the
training ship " Conway," of Liverpool. This was,
of course, the first great step and, at the same time,
greatest event in my early life. Never shall I
forget the first night I passed on board that ship.
I had been brought up, if not in luxury, at any rate
with every comfort that little boys at my age usually
meet. The sudden change, from a comfortable
home and a soft bed and a down pillow to a hard
hammock with no sheets, was very great. Recollect,
too, that I was but twelve years of age. I remember
also, as if it were but yesterday, the first sensation
of getting into bed, or rather, I should say, my new
hammock which served as a bed. I was, I am

told, a good-looking boy, and I had a fair white
skin; and the rough blankets of which my hammock
was composed scrubbed me terribly, not being used
to them. The first night I dared not go to sleep for
fear of falling out; and I am not ashamed to say
that my hammock was moistened with burning
tears, which, at the time, I would rather have died
than allowed the other boys to see. Use, however,
soon became a second nature: in a few weeks' time
I slept as comfortably and securely in my hammock
as ever I did in my little bed at home; and, indeed,
after a long voyage, I often find, the first time I get
into a bed, that the change is such that I cannot
sleep till two or three days have accustomed me
to it.

As may well be imagined, the change of society
on board this training ship was even greater
than the change I experienced in sleeping and
in eating. We varied in age from twelve to sixteen. Though many of the boys were highly
respectable, some were highly the opposite. I
have since, however, in the course of my travels,
heard of schools almost entirely confined to the upper
classes, and I can honestly say, I don't think that
much that was bad which took place on board the
" Conway " was one whit worse than what I know
occurs in many of the highest class schools in this
country.

Let me advise any boy who may read these

lines as follows : if you firmly make up your mind that you will never tell a lie, not only to your master, but to your schoolfellows, I will undertake to say that in less than six months you will be thoroughly respected by all around you. I wish it were in my power to give boys advice as to their conduct in many other matters. Recollect a school is a little world, and probably your conduct in your school will be a guide as to what your conduct will be in after-life. I would, however, quote the following lines, which I recollect reading in that admirable book for boys, " Tom Brown's School Days" :—"And now, Tom, my boy," said the Squire, " remember you are going at your own earnest request to be chucked into this great school like a young bear, with all your troubles before you, earlier than we should have sent you perhaps. If schools are what they were in my time, you will see a great many cruel, blackguard things done, and hear a deal of foul, bad talk. But never fear. You tell the truth, keep a brave and kind heart, and never listen to or say anything you wouldn't have your mother and sister hear, and you will never feel ashamed to come home, or we to see you." I wish these noble words could be deeply engraven on every child's heart when he first leaves home.

Another point that boys should bear in mind at school is, that there is a great distinction between being quarrelsome and being plucky. I have no hesitation in saying, that the boy who will never fight will be sure to get bullied. I would, however, remind my young readers of the excellent advice of Polonius to his son: "Beware of entrance to a quarrel; but, being in, bear it that the opposer may beware of thee."

I remained on board the "Conway" two years; and at the age of fourteen took my first voyage to sea on board a ship called the "Cavour," and sailed in her for Calcutta. Now I do not think that any of you will consider me as a particularly delicate man, nor am I deficient in personal strength. I trust, therefore, some of you boys who are so fond of a good night's rest, and feel so sleepy in the morning that you will run the risk of being punished for being late for breakfast, will remember that I, at the age of fourteen, commenced the ordinary sailor's life, which means that we never have more than four hours' sleep at one time. I was told by Mr. Smith, of University College Hospital, Gower Street, who examined me after my swim across the Channel, that he believed more than six hours' sleep at a time to be absolutely injurious. Of course, it is a subject on which I am quite incapable of giving an opinion. As it would be affectation in me to say that I am not possessed of great powers of endurance, I simply record the fact for the benefit of boys throughout the country, many of whom feel it to be the ambition of their lives to be strong and healthy

men. I say I record the fact that since I was
fourteen years of age I have never had more than
four hours' sleep at a time, as a rule. On the other
hand, I believe I was possessed of an extremely strong
constitution. This showed itself on my very first
voyage. At starting we had extremely bad and
rough weather, so much so that we were fourteen
days in accomplishing the first hundred miles. For
the first time in my life I experienced what a storm
at sea was, and how far different it was to what I had
a few years before pictured to myself, lying in my
little bed at home. However, I was never sea-sick in
my life, and I am thankful to say that I was spared
the misery and right-down agony that I have
often witnessed young lads undergo when at sea
for the first time. I was very small for my age, and
remained so till I was nearly eighteen, when I
began to grow rapidly; and I really do not think
that I ceased growing till I was twenty-five years
of age.

I was apprenticed for three years to Messrs.
Rathborne Brothers, Liverpool, and sailed in
their ship, "Cavour," to Calcutta. From Calcutta
we sailed to Hongkong; and it was at this latter
place that my first real adventure occurred.
Being a lad, young, and full of self-confidence, I
asked to be allowed to go on shore, without, however, having the sense to make inquiries beforehand
as to what parts of the town it was desirable to

visit, and what not. Now Hongkong contains what
may be called the native part, and very few young
men are imprudent enough to go about alone in this
quarter of the town. I had at the time one dollar
in my waistcoat pocket, and I strolled right into the
middle of this part of the town, where it was not
safe even for a full-grown man to go by himself.
I was instantly seized by two Chinamen, who
attempted to search my pockets. I honestly confess that I was horribly frightened ; but, at the same
time, I firmly resolved I would part with my dollar
only with my life. I grasped it firmly in my hand
outside my waistcoat, and, with the other one, I
struck my assailants with all my might. I must
confess that I kicked also, and bit. My assailants
used their utmost strength, which, however, was not
sufficient to capture my solitary dollar. The
struggle lasted for over a quarter of an hour, and
under the influence of my kicks my opponents gave
vent to some uncouth sounds—as well they might,
for Chinamen's shins are by no means tough—which
sounds I presume to have been Chinese oaths.
However, perhaps fortunately, they were unintel-
ligible to me. On a policeman making his appearance
in the distance, my assailants flung me down a steep
embankment, at the bottom of which an open drain
ran. I was fortunate enough to jump the ditch; and
after scrambling up the other side, I made the best
use of my legs and rejoined my ship, none the

poorer for my adventure, though as I said before, I was terribly frightened. Considering my size and age, and that my opponents were two full-grown men, I do not think that we need have any fear in case of another Chinese war.

I have since had considerable experience of Chinamen, and, leaving weapons out of the question, I would willingly undertake to fight at least three at once with my bare fists. I am quite certain, if I could arm my old schoolfellows on board the "Conway," whose ages varied from twelve to sixteen, with some sword-bayonets, that I would lead them to a successful charge against any Chinese regiment that could be brought before them. It would be a happy moment in my life, if ever I got the chance of so doing. The probability is, however, that on the first sound of that "Hip, hip, hurrah!" which cannot be translated into any foreign language, that would assuredly burst from the boys' lips, the regiment opposite would throw down their arms and run like sheep. There is a story on record, that two hundred blue-jackets from a man-of-war were landed somewhere, and that a detachment of Chinese troops, in number about ten thousand, threw down their arms, and took to their heels. I cannot, however, vouch for the accuracy of the story.

From Hongkong we sailed to Singapore, and from Singapore back to Calcutta, and from thence home. The whole voyage occupied me about seventeen months. Of course, I had to undergo all the little experiences which a young lad like myself going to sea for the first time has to put up with; and I would advise any of my young friends who may read this book to remember that the more good-tempered you are, and the more you put up with the fun of your companions on board a ship, the better will you be treated. I had of course to undergo the operation of being "shaved" on my first crossing the Line, though I was not green enough to go on deck and look out for the Line with a telescope, notwithstanding some on board attempted to take me in.

On my return to England, of course I visited my native place, and the universal opinion among my friends was, that the seventeen months of exposure to the sea-air and salt water, with but little sleep— for, as I told you before, we were never allowed more than four hours' sleep at a time—had made quite a man of me. I was not, however, allowed to remain long idle at home, and I soon had to start on my second voyage in the same vessel, the places visited this time being Aden and Bombay. Nothing that occurred during my second voyage that I can now recollect would, I think, interest you. About this time I applied myself, to the best of my ability, to the study of navigation. My third voyage was made in a ship called the "Hampden," and we visited the same places as in the previous voyage. I am not sure, but I think making two voyages in

succession to the same place is a great assistance
in learning, as, in calculating the ship's course, it
seems easier, having been over exactly the same
ground before.   Consequently, it was after this third
voyage that I was enabled to pass my examination,
and obtained a certificate as second mate.   I obtained
a berth as second mate after this, in a ship called the
" Castleton," and in her visited Japan and
Yokohama.

I have visited in the course of my life so many
places—India, China, New York, Valparaiso, Africa,
Singapore, Ceylon, etc.—that to give a detailed
list of all my voyages would be both tedious and
uninteresting.   I will, therefore, pick out a few of
what I consider the most interesting personal adventures in my life, more especially those connected
with the subject of which this book treats.

At one period, I was stationed for a short time
at Port Natal, which, as you probably all know,
is on the South Coast of Africa, and I assisted
in recovering a cargo of a ship that had been
wrecked, and had struck on a shoal some short
distance from land, the distance being about half-
a-mile from shore.   In order to communicate with
the shore through the surf, a large boat had to
be drawn along what is called " the surf-line,"
this "surf-line" consisting of a rope, one end of
which is fastened to the wreck and the other to
the shore.   A number of natives assisted in

the management of this boat, but at night it was necessary, in order to keep her properly afloat, that she should be anchored out close by the wreck. For this purpose I took the last trip out in the boat, and having fastened her, I swam back through the surf. I mention this fact, as it has often been remarked that the natives are extraordinary fine performers in the water. In this particular instance, however, not one of them was sufficiently powerful to swim in the surf at the time I mention, nor do I think that any of the sailors there could have got back through the sea. I may add that I was paid one pound a day for my being able to perform what others could not do, and, considering the risk I ran of being carried out to sea altogether, I do not think that those who employed me had much cause for complaint.

The event of my life which first brought my name in any way before the public in connection with swimming took place on board the Cunard vessel "Russia," which sailed between New York and Liverpool. We were on our homeward voyage when, one day, while a tremendous heavy sea was causing the ship to roll in a manner which rendered it almost impossible for one to keep their feet without a life-line, a cry suddenly arose, "A man overboard." A poor young fellow, Michael Hynes by name, who had been ordered aloft in the main rigging to "clear the sheet," had missed his hold, and fell

B

backwards into the water. I myself saw him fall,
and within two or three seconds I was in the water,
but, alas! nothing could I see of him save his cap.
It was generally supposed afterwards that, in falling,
he must have been struck by the propeller, and have
gone down upon the spot. As I have remarked, the
sea was very rough, and the ship was going at full
speed. I was in the water thirty-seven minutes
before I was picked up by a life-boat which was
lowered for the purpose. I had nothing, however,
but the poor fellow's cap to bring with me. For
this attempt to save life, I received a gold medal
from the Royal Humane Society of London. This
medal, which is perhaps better known as the
"Stanhope Gold Medal," is annually presented by
the trustees of the Royal Humane Society to anyone who, in the course of the year, should, in their
opinion, perform the best act in connection with
saving human life; and I shall always look back
upon being the recipient of the first gold medal ever
given away as one of the most fortunate coincidences
in what, I am bound now to admit, has been a
somewhat fortunate career. In addition to this gold
medal—which, on the occasion of the Royal Humane
Society's dinner, was presented to me in person by
the Duke of Edinburgh—I received another medal
from the Liverpool Humane Society; and the
passengers on board the "Russia" showed their
liberality by collecting for me the sum of £100.

Strange to say, my first swimming opponent was
a Newfoundland dog. A gentleman residing at
Southsea was fond of boasting of the extraordinary
power of his dog in the water. I backed myself,
however, to remain in the water longer than the dog.
The day I chose was rather rough, and a chopping
sea is not adapted for a dog's style of swimming.
I had no difficulty myself in remaining in the water
an hour and a-half, by which time the poor brute
was nearly drowned. Considering how kind the
Royal Humane Society had been to me, I think I
ought to add that I was determined, had the poor
brute sunk, to swim back to the shore with it.
Considering how often Newfoundland dogs have
saved human lives, I do think that one good turn
deserves another. The dog, however, showed its
sagacity by swimming back to the boat in which its
master was seen, and made efforts to climb up the
side. I do not know what period a Newfoundland
dog can remain in the water, but I am disposed
to think their wonderful power of endurance has
been greatly over-rated.

The first time the idea of swimming across the
Channel entered my head was on reading in one of
the papers (I forget which) an account of the attempt
Johnson made to swim from Dover to Calais. The
attempt in question had been well called a " Strange
Affair." Early last year I went down to Dover with
the special purpose of seeing what I could do. I

B 2

hired a small boat, and, with two men to accompany me, I swam across in the direction of France, without, however, having any intention of going the whole distance, even had I felt capable of so doing. On this occasion I swam out as far as the Varne Buoy, which is about ten miles off Folkestone, and, I should think, though I am speaking only from memory, about mid-Channel. I remained in the water four hours and a-half, so it will be seen I was materially assisted by the tide. My first public swim—I mean that which has been noticed by the different newspapers—was on the 3rd of July, when I swam from Blackwall Pier to Gravesend, a distance of twenty miles, of course with the tide. I succeeded in accomplishing this distance in four hours forty-two minutes forty-four seconds, and as I did not experience any difficulty on the point of cold, this success greatly encouraged me in making the attempt to swim across the Channel. I consequently, soon afterwards, proceeded to Dover and commenced practising, remaining in the salt water a longer and longer period every day. I took what may be called a trial trip, and swam from Dover to Ramsgate, remaining on that occasion in the water nearly nine hours. I had now publicly announced my intention of attempting to swim to Calais, and several gentlemen kindly came forward and promised to assist me in my attempt. I had, of course, an immense amount of assistance in the

shape of good advice, and a number of extraordinary
precautions were recommended to me. I was very
strongly advised to cover my body with a coating of
some kind of grease, and, on my swimming to Ramsgate, the grease I used was cod-liver oil. On my
first attempt to swim the Channel I used porpoise
oil, which was recommended to me by the Editor of
Land and Water, who sent me a pot for the purpose,
and whose kindness was not limited to "grease,"
but took the practical form of putting me on £50 to
nothing in case of success. I will not, however, here
enter into the whole details of my Channel swim.
Further on in the book will be found an account by
an eye-witness, giving a far better description than I
myself could possibly give, and to that account I
will refer you. I can only say that the moment
when I touched the Calais sands, and felt the French
soil beneath my feet, is one which I shall never
forget, were I to live for a hundred years. I was
terribly exhausted at the time, and during the last
two or three hours I began to think that, after all, I
should fail. On the following day, after I had had a
good night's rest, I did not feel very much the worse
for what I had undergone. I had a peculiar sensation in my limbs, somewhat similar to that which is
often felt after the first day of the cricket season;
and it was a week before I could wear a shirt-collar,
owing to a red raw rim at the back of my neck,
caused by being obliged to keep my head back for so

long a period ; for, it must be remembered, I was in the water for very nearly twenty-two hours.

In offering the present book to the public, and, with it, giving a short account of my own life, I trust I may be pardoned for any appearance of boastfulness in what I have recorded. I have, however, honestly endeavoured to state simply the facts that have occurred, in the hope that others may, perhaps, profit by my experience. I know full well, having performed an act like mine, how great an influence I must necessarily have upon the minds of young lads, and I would wish to say a few words in conclusion that may possibly be of benefit to them. I know full well how great are the temptations to which young men engaged in a seafaring life are almost invariably exposed at every port at which they land. Comparing the present time with years gone by (and I judge of what my own experience has been compared with the stories that I have been told by men who have got gray in the service), I believe an immense amount of good has been done to sailors by the establishment of Sailors' Homes, which are now so universally to be met with in nearly all great British ports both at home and abroad, I believe an extension of such genuine harbours of refuge would tend greatly to improve the condition of our seamen both mentally and bodily.

I have, of course, since what I may call the event of my life, had ample opportunity for witnessing

almost every style of swimming as shown by the best
swimmers of the day; and I sincerely trust that the
hints and directions that I have given will be instructive, not only in enabling many to learn to
swim, but also in improving both in style and in
endurance many who can already swim a little. I
hope the time will, before long, come when no boy
can say, "I cannot swim," without the same blush
of shame with which an ordinary English schoolboy
would say, "I cannot play cricket," or, "I cannot
catch a ball," or, "I dare not fight." When once
this feeling is universal among young lads, we shall
soon be a nation of swimmers.

CHAPTER I.

BREAST STROKE.

THERE is no doubt that swimming is much easier learned in youth than in middle age; and the younger a lad is, the easier it is for him to learn. Of all places for this purpose, I believe that none will be found better than a bath. It will always be found that, where the water is warm, it is much easier to remain in a long period than where the water is cold. It is for this reason that all our fast swimmers come from inland towns. Boys at the sea have, probably, but a few weeks or, at the outside, a few months in the course of the year in which they find it practicable to go into the water. Rough days, cold weather, too often deter lads from bathing, though cases are, indeed, occasionally found in which men will bathe in the sea all the year round, not only in mid-summer but in mid-winter as well.

In commencing, therefore, to teach a person to swim, the first point is, entering the water. Now, where the learner is very young, very often the

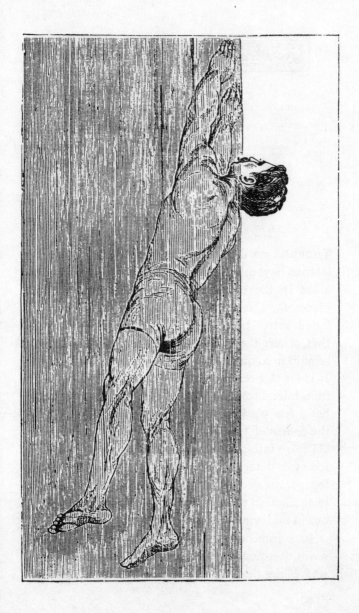

greatest difficulty is to induce him to enter the water at all. I recollect a case some years ago in which a lad, described by his parents as "somewhat delicate," was sent to me to learn to swim. For the first three days I could not get him even to take off his clothes, and after a time, when I induced him to undress, he used to cling to one of the posts of the bath, and screamed every time I tried to get him into the water. Of course, in a case like this, teaching is hopeless until the boy has been taught to overcome his fears. On the other hand, when you find the case of a lad who will boldly plunge in the first time, you may rest assured that he will be found to learn to swim in a very short period. It was in the same bath and the same year that another boy, who was sent to me to learn to swim, boldly plunged off the diving board into six feet of water, and trusted to me to catch him, which I had no difficulty in doing. In the case of this boy, I found that at the end of three days he was able to swim twenty yards. In the case of teaching very young children, they should be treated similarly as you would treat a puppy-dog. Once frighten the child, and the effect will be exactly the same as with a young dog. They will never enter the water again, if they can help it. Now, in the case of teaching children of five or six years of age, there is no doubt that the best place where they can learn is in a large pool at the seaside at low tide. A child can be gradually induced to go deeper and deeper; salt water being more buoyant than fresh, any child will float on his back the first time. The effect of this floating is, that the child instantly gains confidence. Even in a bath in which the water is tepid, a child, especially if he be a chubby one, will be found to float with ease. In the case of boys from ten to sixteen, as a rule no difficulty will be found in inducing them to enter the water. Still, however, great differences in character will be observed, as some seem physically incapable of remaining in the water at starting. How often will you find a boy, when he first enters the water, instantly clutch at the steps or edge of the bath, and that all his breath seems to have left his body. This is partially nervousness, partially weakness; and in these cases nothing can be done in the way of teaching until the boy overcomes the difficulty of breathing, and is able to walk about freely within his depth without catching hold of the side.

Having once persuaded a pupil to walk about within his depth, the next great point is to prove to him how great is the buoyancy of the water. I think it will be found that, in almost all works written on the subject of swimming, the same plan is recommended, viz., to place some object at the bottom of the bath (such as a large stone or piece of white chalk), and then to tell the pupil to pick it up with his hand. He will now experience the difficulty, not of keeping himself up, but of getting down. The buoyancy of the water is so great that, supposing him to be about chest deep, probably he will be unable to pick up the stone at all. He will now find from this how very little is necessary to keep a man afloat.

Another good plan sometimes is: let some person go into the water with the beginner, and float on his back, resting on the learner's hand. Then tell him to take his hand away for a second or two at a time, and, so to speak, balance the body on his hand. He will find the pressure of the body barely that of a few ounces. In fact, the human body is so nearly the same weight as an equal bulk of water, that the movement of the arms and legs in swimming is not necessary so much to keep the body afloat as to keep it afloat in the right position. Many a drowning man has come repeatedly to the surface, but often, unfortunately, the mouth or nose, through which he could breathe, has not been the portion that reached the surface. Another method by which you can give your pupil confidence is to go into the water yourself, and to prove to him by ocular demonstration how very slight a movement of the limbs is necessary to keep the body afloat and to keep the mouth above the water. All good swimmers know how very little movement of the hands or feet will be sufficient for this purpose.

In commencing to learn to swim, all boys should first learn to swim well on their chests. Since the introduction of the side stroke, it will be often found that lads, who have barely learned to swim properly at all, try to imitate the first-class professionals, and in so doing succeed simply in making themselves ridiculous. Any day, on visiting a London bath, it will be found that some puny, sickly child may be seen attempting to swim what he imagines to be the side stroke; his tiny arm will be flashing in the air like the sails of a windmill, and the boy's head bobbing up and down in the water, very little progress being made. Now for a side stroke to be at all effective, it is essential that a first-class stroke with the legs be first acquired.

I recollect reading in a weekly journal, a few months ago, a very true illustration of this point. The writer had visited the Lambeth Baths, and had, by means of his watch, timed for several lengths a little boy who had been trying to swim on his side, the boy leaving off after each length. The same boy was afterwards asked to swim on his chest the same distance, namely, one length of the bath. Then, as the writer had imagined, swimming on his chest, the boy went several seconds faster than he did when swimming on his side. Now, to swim well on the chest, the greatest difficulty at starting will be found in the management of the legs. The movement of the arms is a natural one, but the movement of the legs unnatural. Hence the difficulty human beings find in swimming, which is, so far as I know, not experienced by any animal. The movement of the limbs of a dog in the water are very similar to the movement of his limbs on shore; but the movement of the legs in the case of a good swimmer is one that cannot be acquired in a day. It will often be found at starting a good plan for the pupil to catch hold of, say, the side of the bath or the steps, or in fact any object that is stationary, and for the teacher to enter the water and slowly to move the pupil's legs in the proper direction.

The great secret of a good stroke is to kick out the legs wide; and here let me observe that it is a popular fallacy to imagine that the speed of the swimmer in any way depends upon the resistance of the water against the soles of the feet. I have often heard it observed: "Oh! that man would make a fine swimmer; he has got such large feet." Now, in the movement of the legs, the flat of the foot never directly meets the water, except in the case which I shall hereafter mention, known as "treading water." The propelling power in swimming is caused by the legs being suddenly brought from a position in which they are placed wide apart into one in which they close together like the blades of a pair of scissors. In fact, the mechanical power here brought into play is that of the wedge. For instance, suppose a wedge of ice were suddenly pinched hard between the thumb and finger, it is

evident that the wedge of ice would shoot off in the
direction opposite to that in which the sharp edge
points. Now in bringing the legs suddenly together,
so to speak, a wedge of water is forced backwards,
and the resistance caused propels the body forward
in exactly an opposite direction. When this point
is well considered, the importance of drawing the
legs well up will at once become manifest. Should
anyone stand and catch hold of a chair or a table,
and draw one of their feet up, say, half-a-yard, and
then kick, how feeble will that kick be. Should
they, however, draw their foot up till it nearly
touches their body, how powerful a kick can then
be given. The learner should, from the very first,
continually keep this point in view. Too often a
swimmer will be found whose stroke with his legs
consists of a series of spasmodic jerks, probably
four times quicker, and with quite four times as
much work as the powerful leg stroke of a first-class
performer. The beginner having practised to move
his legs properly in the way we have suggested,
namely, by catching hold of some object with his
hands, he had next best try a few strokes in which
he uses his hands as well as his legs. Unfortunately,
he will here probably experience a check. The
moment he tries to move his hands, he will find
that his legs seem to refuse to obey his wishes.
This is but natural. Let one sit on a chair, and
try and move their right leg round one way, and

their right arm round the other. The difficulty of doing this will show the difficulty that the beginner in swimming feels in the water by having one movement with his legs and a different one with his arms. Patience and perseverance will, however, soon overcome this difficulty.

We have already explained that the proper movement for the legs in swimming is to draw them both well up till the heel, if possible, touches the body, and then strike them well out right and left, exactly as if the swimmer wished to kick a man standing at his right and left hand at the same moment, then bring the legs well together, till the heels touch each other and the toes point backwards. In drawing up the legs, it should also be remembered that the toes should be pointed. By this means the resistance of the water against the insteps of the feet, which resistance would retard the swimmer, is avoided. Again, too, in dwelling on the stroke (and by dwelling on the stroke, we mean resting for a few seconds in the water while the body moves forward) care should be taken that the toes are pointed in a direction directly contrary to that in which the swimmer is going. The movement of the arms is never one in which great difficulty will be found. The two hands should be kept perfectly flat, the palms resting on the water; and at the same time, as the swimmer strikes out with his legs, each hand should be brought slowly round, one to the right, the other to the left, care being taken that the palm of the hand is horizontal. Were the hands to be placed sideways, it is at once evident that the water would offer but little resistance. By keeping the hands in the position we have named, the resistance offered by the water, in case of sinking, would be very considerable. Should the beginner doubt this, let him enter the water and stoop down, and keeping his hand flat, bring it suddenly downwards in the water, the resistance that the water will offer prevents him doing this with any speed at all. On the other hand, should he strike downwards with his hand sideways, he will find that he can do it as fast almost as he could in the air.

Now, in reaching forward with the hands, the swimmer should always endeavour to reach as far forward as possible. Let him imagine some small object is placed in the water just out of reach, and let him struggle to reach it; the more he reaches forward the faster will he swim. This is a very important point, which we will have to consider at greater length when we come to speak of the over-hand stroke. I would strongly recommend every boy learning to swim to be very particular as to the kind of stroke he acquires with his legs. Bear in mind that, if once you get into a bad style, you will experience ten times the difficulty in altering it into a correct one, than you would by commencing to learn to swim afresh; for this reason I would recommend, if possible, everyone learning to swim to go and watch carefully some first-class swimmer, to see how he moves his legs, and then imitate him as closely as possible. Many boys, self-taught, swim in a style peculiar to themselves. They jerk themselves along in the water, but by means of strokes which it would be absolutely impossible to keep up long. Now, in beginning to swim, the point to be primarily borne in view is not so much to be able to swim very fast for a short distance, and then be obliged to stop, as to be able to continue swimming steadily for a long period.

I have been told by many who are considered good judges of swimming that my late feat, as it is called, of swimming across the Channel will be probably productive of much good in calling attention to this point. Recollect that, in the course of your future lives, if any of you get upset in a boat or wrecked at sea, you will have to depend upon saving your life by means of a slow, steady stroke. The stroke known as the overhand stroke is well adapted to go very fast for a short distance in a bath, but it would be wholly impossible to swim in that style in a rough sea, and in a suit of clothes. I do not wish for one moment to cry down the professional style of swimming of the day, but I would remind my readers that, just as to be able to march forty miles with a knapsack on one's back in reasonable time is far more useful for the soldier than to be able to run a hundred yards in, say, ten seconds ; so to be able to swim five to ten miles in a suit of clothes is far more practically useful than to be able to swim 500 yards in seven minutes, if such time be possible.

Swimming should be regarded throughout the country not as a means to win a medal or to win a cup, but as an art which every boy and every man should know in reference to the saving of human life. Still, it is quite possible to combine the two qualities—endurance and speed. But I would strongly urge upon all lads beginning to swim, that they should make themselves perfectly masters of a good, strong, steady stroke, which they can keep up for half-an-hour, before they commence learning the side stroke; and I have no hesitation in saying, that if they ever wish really to be proficient at the side stroke, they cannot do better than patiently learn to swim on their chest first. To attempt to swim on the side, before one can swim well on the chest, is as ridiculous as to make a child run before it can walk.

Another important point to be considered in swimming in any position is the position of the body in the water. Now it is evident that the body should be kept as much as possible, horizontal. The swimmer should therefore throw himself on his chest, and endeavour to keep his heels as near the top of the water as possible, at the same time keeping them in the water. If two small sticks of wood be placed in any piece of still water, the one floating horizontally, and the other having one end heavier than the other—consequently being in a slanting position—by giving the same impulse to each, it will at once become apparent that the horizontal position offers far less resistance than that of the slanting one. Again, if the body be kept horizontal, the movements of the arms and legs tend to propel the body through the water. If the body be kept too much in a slanting position, the movements of the arms and legs tend to force the body out of the water. The difference between a good and bad swimmer will be then found that, the former goes through the water, the latter bobs up and down in the water.

Now let us for one moment consider the position of the hands, more especially that of the thumb and fingers. It is evident that our object should be to offer as much resistance to the water as possible. The thumb, therefore, should be placed by the side of the first finger, and not underneath it. It has often, too, been argued that the fingers should be kept close together; this, however, is a fallacy, and one which a few moments' consideration will be sufficient to dispel. The resistance offered by the hand with the fingers open must of necessity be as great, if not greater, than the resistance opposed to the water with the fingers shut; and in swimming, especially in long distances, it will be found a relief to open the fingers, since to keep the hands very long in one position is very conducive to cramp.

A very common fault with beginners is that they endeavour too much to keep their heads out of the water, and consequently the greater efforts will they be forced to make to keep themselves afloat. Those efforts, therefore, will be wasted in keeping the body up which might be used in propelling the body forward. Every movement in the water should be directed towards propelling the body forward. The natural buoyancy of the body is in itself sufficient to keep it afloat. As long as the head is sufficiently out of the water to breathe at the moment of drawing in the breath, all that is requisite will be done.

Those who recollect Harry Gurr will remember how he used to swim in the water, and go through it rather than on it, bringing his mouth to the surface with a twist to breathe, more like the hippopotamus in the Zoological Gardens, that comes up occasionally with a great snort. Of course, swimming of this description is totally impossible in a chopping sea; but, without going so far as to say that a swimmer should keep his head under water, I will warn him against being too much afraid of the water touching his face.

I believe it to be in the power of everyone with fairly healthy lungs to teach themselves to swim; but at the same time I cannot too strongly urge on them the importance, if possible, of witnessing a perfect model.

I would very strongly warn boys against learning to swim in rivers where there is a running stream and deep pools. Many a life has been lost in streams by boys who were capable of making a few strokes, in doing which they have been carried down the stream, and suddenly found themselves out of their depth. Considering how easy it is in all parts of the country for bathing places to be filled up by means of open gratings in the rivers, those bathing accidents which are so constantly occurring are no less than a national disgrace. Of course, in rivers where there is a tide there is more difficulty, as the expense of a bathing place is necessarily considerable. But in streams that maintain nearly the same level all the year round, the expense of forming a suitable bathing place for lads is so trifling, that in the neighbourhood of all large towns and villages the erection of such bathing places ought to be compulsory.

I will now presume that my pupil has sufficiently mastered the breast stroke to be able to swim without distress for at least a quarter of an hour, and will proceed to describe as correctly as possible the side stroke, and afterwards the overhand stroke.

CHAPTER II.

SIDE STROKE.

THERE are many persons who do not understand the difference between the side stroke and the overhand stroke. We will briefly state, by way of commencement, that the difference between the two is as follows. In both styles of swimming, the swimmer is on his side. In the ordinary side stroke, the upper hand, or rather the upper arm, is brought forward in the water; in the overhand stroke the upper hand is brought forward out of the water. First, then, let us consider the ordinary side stroke, and we have already supposed that the swimmer is sufficiently proficient on his chest to be able to swim at least ten minutes or a quarter of an hour without stopping.

We will first suppose the swimmer to swim on his right side, though it should be borne in mind that a good side-stroke swimmer is able to swim on either side, and we would recommend beginners to practise both positions for the following great advantage. In any race it is very important that the swimmer should be able to see his opponent. Now it is evident that, unless a man can swim on both sides, in swim-

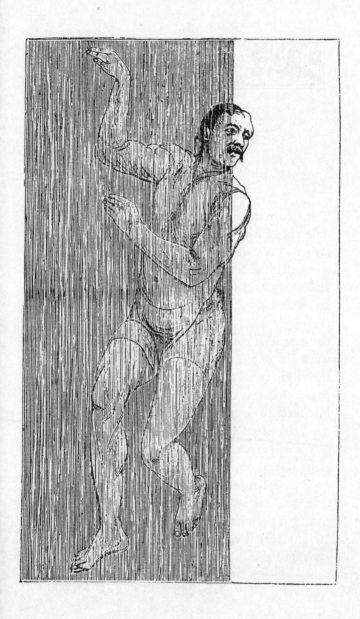

ming in a bath, in which he has to turn, he will only
see his opponent half the time; and it is for this reason that, in tossing for the choice of sides before a
race, anyone who is more proficient on one side than
the other invariably chooses that side which would
enable him to see his opponent the last length they
have to swim.

To commence swimming on the side, the first
thing the swimmer will have to do is to throw himself, say, on his right side, and to reach forward his
right arm in the water, keeping his hand flat, precisely as he did when swimming on his chest. To
keep the same stroke with his legs as in the breast
stroke, the left arm is now brought forward through
the water a little to the left of the swimmer's head.
The head is so placed that the right cheek rests on
the water. The movement of the right arm is partially downwards and partially backwards. The
downward movement assists to keep the head above
water; the backward movement propels the body
forward; and at the finish of the stroke the movement of the right hand should be as if the swimmer
had grasped a handful of water and had thrown it
in the direction of his feet. For this to be of service in propelling the body forward, it is essential
that the body should be kept in as horizontal a
position as possible. The movement of the left
arm is, when the swimmer has reached as far
forward in the water as he can, a little to the left

of his head, and grasped in imagination a handful of water, he must bring the left arm back
with a quick sharp movement through the water,
throwing the handful in the direction of his feet. In
swimming on the side, the head during the whole
time is partially submerged, and some little care will
be requisite at starting to avoid taking in a mouthful
of water. In a warm tepid bath, where the water is
not changed too often, this is an exceedingly dis-
agreeable *contretemps*. In a rough sea this style of
swimming is barely possible. It is, however, the
most elegant form of swimming of any, and we
would mention as, perhaps, two of the most perfect
models, Beckwith, senior, and David Pamplin.
The body appears to glide through the water at each
stroke, and the greatest care should be exercised to
avoid the too common fault of bobbing up and
down. On a smooth piece of water, such as the
Serpentine, two swimmers, such as I have mentioned, viewed from a distance, look like two black balls
shooting at the rate of about a yard a second, slowly
but evenly, through the water. In commencing to
learn this style of swimming, the greatest difficulty
that the beginner will experience is that of knowing
when to draw in his breath; and for this purpose a
slight roll of the head is practised by many, the roll
bringing the mouth higher out of the water. This style
of swimming was very much in vogue from twelve
to fifteen years ago; but of late years has rapidly

given way to the far more effective, and at the same time uglier style, known as the overhand stroke. One advantage that the ordinary side stroke possesses over its faster rival is, that the swimmer is far better able to see the direction in which he is going. When we come to speak of the overhand stroke, we shall have more to say on this subject.

We have before warned beginners that they must learn to walk before they can run; and we would here strongly recommend them before they commence the overhand stroke, as they probably will do, especially if they are boys, for some time to practise the good old-fashioned side stroke which, we can assure them, has brought in many first-class men in races in years gone by. When we say that the movement with the legs is exactly the same as swimming on the chest, we would warn beginners against the too common fault of kicking one leg a little bit out of the water. The left leg, should the swimmer be swimming on the right side, is obviously placed higher than the right, and care must be taken that the foot does not occasionally shoot out of the water. When this is the case, the whole power of the leg stroke is, of course, lost. I would mention an instance—a very common one—when this is likely to occur. We all know salt water is far more buoyant than fresh. Those who doubt the fact should take two tumblers, one filled with salt water and the other with fresh.

A small piece of amber, whose specific gravity is very nearly the same as that of water, will float in the one, but sink in the other. Again, tepid water is slightly less buoyant than cold. A swimmer, therefore, who has been accustomed for many years to swim in a tepid water bath, should bear in mind, when he reaches the sea, and swims in it for the first time, that his whole body will be placed slightly higher than it was in fresh, and consequently he runs far more danger of kicking one leg out of the water than he did before. It is for this same reason (the greater buoyancy of the water) that it is easier to swim for a longer time in salt water than in fresh. When I swam across the Channel, I remained for nearly twenty-two hours in the water. I confess that I do not think I could remain nearly so long in fresh water, as the exertion necessary to keep myself afloat would be far greater in the latter case than in the former.

CHAPTER III.

OVERHAND STROKE.

WE will now proceed to the overhand stroke. There is no doubt that this stroke is by far the most effective; but at the same time, there can be no doubt whatever that it is far more exhausting than either the side or breast stroke. As we mentioned before, the only difference between the overhand stroke and the side stroke is that, in the former the upper arm is brought forward out of the water; that is, if the swimmer swims on his right side, the right hand, as in the side stroke, is thrown forward in the water, but the left arm is brought forward out of the water, and stretched forward as far as the swimmer can possibly reach in the direction in which he is going, a few inches in front of his face; the water is here grasped by the hand, the thumb being kept out and the hand brought back by a rapid, strong pulling movement, the water being thrown in the direction contrary to that in which the swimmer is going. Now, the advantage of bringing forward the arm out of the water instead of in it will be at once obvious by a few minutes' considera-

D

tion. Just as, in rowing, the oarsman feathers his
oar in order to avoid the resistance of the air
against the flat of the blade, so does the swimmer
bring forward his arm out of the water in order to
avoid the resistance that bringing the arm forward
in the midst of the water would necessarily cause.
Any movement in the water in any one direction has
a tendency to cause the body to move in exactly the
contrary direction. Therefore, in bringing the arm
forward in the water, the natural tendency is to stop
the body's moving; by bringing forward the arm
out of the water, this retarding movement is avoided.
At the same time, however, it should be borne
in mind that, by bringing the arm out of the water,
there is a tendency to sink the body. Unless, therefore, the pupil be a powerful swimmer, it is mere
folly to make him attempt this stroke at all. The
natural consequence of raising the arm is, of course,
to sink the head ; and, if any one watches first-class
model swimmers, probably the first impression will
be that they seem to go through the water rather
than on it ; and it is often a matter of marvel to
many to see how the swimmer breathes at all. Of
course, swimmers vary. H. Gurr, who was the
first to bring the overhand stroke to perfection,
seemed to bring his mouth to the surface occasionally when he wished it, and remain under the
water the rest of the time, nothing being seen
beyond a powerful arm flourishing out of the water.

In bringing forward the upper arm, care should be taken not to bring it forward like the sail of a windmill going round, but to throw the arm forward and to reach as far forward as possible. Just as, in swimming on the chest, we wanted the arms to be thrown well forward, so in swimming on the side, in this overhand stroke, the endeavour of the swimmer each time he moves his arm should be, so to speak, to overreach himself. Let him imagine some object is placed in front of him which he is barely able to reach, and let him each time make an effort to touch it. By this means he will find that he swims faster. To my mind, the greatest drawback to the overhand stroke is the extraordinary difficulty the swimmer has in seeing where he is going.

My young friend Baker, who accompanied me across the Channel—and who I have no doubt would have dived for me, had his services been required, which, I am thankful to say, was not the case—told me that he lost a race down at Ryde owing to his mistaking his course. Instead of swimming to the pier, he went straight out to sea; and, though far superior to any of the boys with whom he competed, came in last of all. Then, it should be borne in mind, he had been accustomed to swim in a bath, where occasional glimpses of the side of the bath is a guide. In the open sea, unless the swimmer be accompanied by a boat, it is almost impossible to keep a correct course while swimming the overhand stroke. The

best I have ever witnessed in the sea in this particular style of swimming is Tom Morris.

As I have said before, the overhand stroke is
decidedly the fastest style of swimming that can be
adopted ; but then it is so exhausting, that it is next
to impossible to keep it up for any long period. I
should say that the limit that a man can keep up
swimming in this way would be half-an-hour. Now
to swim one mile in still water in half-an-hour is a
wonderful performance. It has been said that it
has been done, but it has never been properly
authenticated. In a piece of water such as the
Serpentine, where the course is well known and
where any mistake as to distance would be simply
impossible, no one has ever swum at the rate of one
mile in half-an-hour. From what I have heard, I
believe that E. T. Jones, of Leeds, and J. B.
Johnson, who is at present in America, could swim
one mile in still water in half-an-hour. I do not
believe that there is any other swimmer who could
do the same. In judging of the pace at which a
man swims, a very good rough guess is to calculate
at the rate of one yard to the second. It is evident
that this would be very first-class swimming, as one
yard a second is at the rate of one mile a little
under half-an-hour ; and, as I have before said, I do
not think there are any two men in England at the
present time who could perform this feat. Of course
I may be mistaken. A better distance, perhaps, to

judge of swimming is that of 500 yards. Any
amateur who can swim a fairly measured 500
yards in eight minutes is a very first-class
swimmer. Twelve lengths of the Lambeth baths
is about 480 yards. Now many races have taken
place in these baths, but I do not think that
there is any record of the distance having been
swum in seven and a half minutes, except in
the case when Tom Morris swam young Beckwith,
on which occasion Tom Morris did the distance
in seven minutes seventeen seconds. On another
occasion, when Harry Parker swam Dunlop, of
Leeds, about two years ago, at the Wenlock Baths
in the City Road, Harry Parker swam at the rate of
500 yards in seven and a half minutes, though he
did not do it absolutely in that time, as owing to his
having got a considerable distance ahead of his
opponent, he was stopped by his friends and finished
slowly. As there is no doubt, however, that he
could have swum the last two lengths as fast as he
swam the fifth and sixth (the whole distance being
nine lengths of the bath), had he continued swimming
his best, he would, undoubtedly, have done this time.
Probably the fastest swimmer the world has ever
seen is E. T. Jones, of Leeds. I have every reason
for believing that this wonderful swimmer could
swim 500 yards in seven minutes. I should, however, very much like to see it done. Perhaps, before
long, some good annual prize will be offered, which

will enable us to know for certain what these really magnificent swimmers can do.

I will now proceed to explain, as far as my knowledge goes, the best method of training to win a race. Of course one important point to be considered is the distance. To train to swim 500 yards and to train to swim the Channel are two distinctly opposite things, and what would do most good in the one case would probably do harm in the other. To swim 500 yards the only thing to be considered is speed. To swim a long distance, the greatest enemy the swimmer will have to contend against is the cold.

Further on, in the description of my swim across the Channel, it will be seen that I endeavoured to take all the fat and nourishing food I possibly could weeks before I started, and even in mid-Channel I drank a glass of cod-liver oil, as I was informed that oil is the greatest protection against cold. In cold climates, such as the northern parts of Russia, it is a common thing for the poorer classes to drink oil; and there are some amusing stories told of Russian sailors, when they visited England, before the invention of gas, and when our streets were lighted with oil-lamps. Some of these men, it is said, climbed the posts, blew out the lamps, and drank their contents for supper. I recollect as a child reading some stories of the adventures of Arctic expeditions, and hearing that the sailors had been repeatedly known to boil down their tallow candles, and accustom themselves to eat the tallow, because they found it kept them warm. How far these stories are true, I cannot say. However, I devoutly believed them as a boy; but I am sorry to say that, since I have been twice round the world, many of the stories of adventures by sea told me when I was a child, have turned out to have no more foundation than some of the romances of the "Arabian Nights."

But to return to our subject. First let me impress upon you that boys do not require any training at all; and when I say boys, I mean those about seventeen. Training simply means a healthy life. Of course, if a boy of sixteen be foolish enough to have commenced smoking a short pipe and drinking beer, not because he likes it, but because he thinks it manly, the first step he must take will be to stop both these foolish habits; and at his age he will probably find that his vanity will be equally tickled by telling his companion in as manly a tone of voice as possible "that he is in training," as by either smoking his pipe or by drinking his beer, both of which probably, if the truth were known, make him feel somewhat sick. In the case of a full-grown man, to get rid of internal fat by training is of the utmost importance. For instance, a man may commence training weighing twelve stones, and in the course of a few weeks get himself down to ten and a half. A boy of sixteen, who weighs

between seven and eight stone, will probably, with
all his exercises, sweating, etc., weigh rather more
at the end of a couple of months than he did at the
commencement.

For young lads, therefore, I would recommend the
following simple directions.   Go to bed early, say
between ten and eleven, and get up between five and
six, do not smoke, and if you have been accustomed
to drink beer, one glass with your dinner and one
with your supper will be more than sufficient.   If
you have not been accustomed to drink beer, do not
begin it.   Avoid eating indigestible food, such as
nuts, walnuts and sweets, but eat and drink your
breakfast, dinner, tea and supper, as usual.   Avoid
drinking anything between meals, and, before
swimming or any violent exercise, any effervescent
fluid such as ginger beer, lemonade, etc., etc., is
highly objectionable; next, take plenty of exercise
in the open air, and practise daily in the water the
distance you intend swimming.   Suppose this
distance to be 500 yards, you will find that to swim
500 yards every day fast is very exhausting, and
probably after you have done so five or six days
running, you will feel that you don't go so fast as
when you began.   A great deal of this is very
illusory. It will be often found that you do very fast
time, when you yourself in the water think you are
doing very badly.   Should you wish to have what is
generally known as a "trial" (and for the benefit of

those who don't understand the meaning of this
expression, we will explain that to be—doing the
distance in the water at your very best, while some
friend times you with his watch)—if, I say, you wish
to do a trial, it will be best to have one day's
rest beforehand.

It is wonderful, if you have been practising for
some weeks at a long distance, how a day or even
two days' rest improves one. I have known cases
in which, in so short a distance as 500 yards, after
steadily practising, an improvement of as much as
ten seconds has taken place, after giving the wearied
swimmer a rest of a couple of days from entering
the water altogether. Of course, in training, very
much depends upon the constitution; and very
much must be left to the swimmer's own common
sense. It is evidently impossible to train a pale, thin,
delicate young man on the same principle as one
who has a bull neck, a bullet head with sunken eyes
and a jaw like a bull-dog. When you meet a man
in the street whose profession is stamped on his
countenance as that of " a pug.," you will at once see
such a one would undergo three times the amount of
exercise, abstinence from food, and hardship, than
one who in features resembled a Grecian statue could
undergo. Among the mistakes made by young men
at Oxford and Cambridge in the question of training one is that they treat themselves as if they
were prizefighters. Of course their constitutions

break down, and very often get ruined for life. Both are men—we mean the pug. and the under-graduate—but the difference between the two is as truly marked as the difference between the winner of the Derby and a cart-horse. Both are horses, but the one would fail to do a day's ploughing as signally as the other would fail to win the Good-wood Cup.

CHAPTER IV.

TREADING WATER.

By treading water, we mean standing upright in the water, and keeping the head well out, and at the same time, if possible, keeping the arms, or rather hands, out of the water. This is done by a rapid movement of the feet—something like a man on the treadmill, when it is going round very fast. This is somewhat exhausting, and, as I before mentioned, one of the few positions in swimming in which having large flat feet is very serviceable. If a man were "webb-footed"—a joke which has been made so often with regard to myself that I am somewhat tired of it—of course he could tread water easier than one who is not. When I swam across the Channel, I was obliged to tread water every time I took refreshment; one of the stipulations made beforehand being that I was not to touch a boat the whole time from one shore to the other.

Of course, it is a fact that a fat person can maintain this position far easier than one who is thin. Care also should be taken to keep the lungs as

inflated as possible during the whole period. Of
course, when the lungs are inflated the body is far
more buoyant than when the lungs are empty. And
I may here mention that there is a trick which any
person can accomplish with a little practice, namely,
that of lying still at the bottom of the water. In a
bath where the water is very clear, this has an extraordinary effect—I may say a somewhat horrible
effect, as it gives a very vivid idea to the looker-on
of a dead body lying at the bottom of the water.
The way to do this is to throw oneself on one's back,
and with a slight movement of the hands to cause
the body to sink backwards and downwards. At the
last moment empty the lungs of every particle of
air : the lungs being empty, the body slowly sinks,
and remains at the bottom of the water. Of course,
a person can remain there so long as he can refrain
from drawing in his breath. This, however, will
not be any great period ; in fact, barely half the
time that a person can remain in the water in the
ordinary way. In order to remain under water for
any long period, of course a person takes a deep
breath *in* before going down ; and when they have
held the air in their lungs as long as they possibly
can, they can relieve themselves by breathing out,
and then, having remained with the air out of their
lungs as long as possible, they must come to the
surface in order to breathe.

Stories have been told of men remaining in the

water four minutes. I do not believe this to be true, nor will I believe it till I see it done under circumstances which preclude the possibility of any trickery, such as having a belt containing air round the waist, which is supposed to be a heavy belt, in order to enable one to sink. In remaining under water a long time, it will be found a relief at the last moment almost to fill the mouth with water. The reason that this relieves the chest is—the air that was formerly in the mouth is forced into the lungs. Many swimmers who may have experienced the relief I mention are, perhaps, at the same time ignorant of the cause.

CHAPTER V.

DIVING.

DIVING from a height requires, as Artemus Ward observed when he took the census, experience, like any other business; and just as that worthy gentleman got into difficulties with the two first old maids he met, and whose mouths he attempted to examine, not believing their answers to be correct with regard to age, so many a boy who has witnessed the apparently easy feat of taking a header has come to terrible grief by finding himself come down flat on the water, which he has shortly afterwards left with the appearance of having had a particularly strong mustard-poultice on his chest. Now, in diving from a height of say six feet, the heels must be thrown well up, the legs should be kept straight and well together, and the two hands brought forward in front of the head, exactly similar to the position that a man takes in making his first attempt at swimming on his chest. The hands act simply as a breakwater, and they should be turned up the moment the water is reached, thus preventing the diver going deep,

and also enables him to dart forward along the surface the moment he reaches the water. A good
diver can dive from a height of forty to fifty feet, and
yet never go a yard below the surface. One of the
neatest divers I have ever witnessed was young
Baker, who accompanied me across the Channel on
both occasions on which I crossed, and whose services, I have before remarked, I am extremely glad I
did not require.

On one occasion, when only fourteen years of age,
this boy dived from the top deck of Her Majesty's
ship " President," stationed at the West India
Docks. The height above the water was forty-
five feet, and those who witnessed him assured me
that they did not think he went more than two feet
below the surface. I would not, however, recommend anyone, either man or boy, to attempt to dive
from such a height. Were they to slip or to fall
flat, the probability is that they would be killed on
the spot. But should it at any time be necessary to
take a dive from a high place, bear in mind that
you must not give the same movement to your body
as if you were going off from the height of a few
feet, otherwise you will turn completely over in the
air and come down on your back, which, should the
distance be very great, would probably kill you; and
if the distance be moderate, you would certainly
have the appearance of having had a severe whip-
ping. In diving and in everything else, it is practice

only that will make perfect. I have dived off the yard-arm of a ship which is quite thirty feet above the water; but if by chance any one from such a height comes in the least degree flat, he will hurt himself very considerably. There are many stories told of native divers, but this refers merely to their power of remaining under water, and not their diving from a height; and, as far as swimming goes, none of the black people that I have ever seen approach a first-class English swimmer. Though I have said three feet of water are sufficient to dive in, no man in his senses would ever make a dive from any height unless the water were at least five or six feet deep, as if by chance he should come down a little more straight than he intended, he would in-evitably dash his brains out, in addition to breaking both his arms against the bottom of the bath or river. Great care too should be taken in diving into any open piece of water, as I recollect a case in which a man was seen to receive a fearful laceration of his skull from diving on to a broken green glass bottle which had been thrown in.

CHAPTER VI.

SWIMMING THROUGH THE SURF.

It is needless for me to state that swimming
through a rough sea is very different to swimming
in smooth water; and by a rough sea, I do not
mean an ordinary swimming match that takes place
in ordinary weather, but the still more practical art
of going out through a rough surf, or returning
through one. You will remember that, in the short
account I gave of my life, I mentioned a circumstance that occurred at Port Natal, in which I had
to return to shore from the wreck through a heavy
surf. Perhaps very few of you fully realise what a
heavy surf is. Probably all of you have, however,
read that extremely graphic account of Robinson
Crusoe, when he escaped from the wreck on which
all were lost, and he alone succeeded in reaching
the shore. He describes how a huge mass of water
carried him with tremendous speed forward, and
then left him high and dry; but the receding water
again took him off his feet, and carried him out to
sea. The writer of that book must evidently have

E

experienced what a heavy rolling sea really is. The great art in returning to shore is, not to attempt to battle with the waves, but to manœuvre with them so that they assist you. Should a huge mass of water be bearing down upon you from behind, wait till it nearly reaches you, and then suddenly dive downwards, swim a little way under water as far as you can against the waves. By this means you will avoid being caught in the crest of the wave. Then turn again and strike out to shore, and let yourself be carried on the huge bend of the wave which will take you rapidly in. The waves by this means will bring you nearer and nearer the shore; and the nearer you get the greater must your care be that you don't get caught, as I have said, in the crest of the wave, the effect of which will be to dash you on the beach, and probably, at the same time, knock all the breath out of your body. It will generally be found that every third and every ninth wave is larger than the others, and, also, that every large wave is followed by a much smaller one. In reaching the shore, therefore, watch your opportunity, if possible, to land as soon as you can after these great waves have broken.

In swimming out through the surf you must, of course, start in one of these small waves, and when the sea appears to be in its calmest moments. Again, the first time you see a heavy billow higher than the rest rolling with tremendous force towards you, wait till it is nearly on you, then dive quickly and swim with all your might against the water as long as you possibly can, and your head will shoot above water when the wave itself has passed far back behind you. To attempt swimming in a heavy surf would be an act of folly for anyone, however great a swimmer he might be, unless he were possessed of considerable personal strength.

CHAPTER VII.

RECENT REMARKABLE SWIMMING FEATS.

J. B. JOHNSON SWIMMING THE STRAITS.

THE recent exploit of J. B. Johnson at Dover, on Saturday last, though apparently got up for the same purpose as his former one at London Bridge, viz., that of bringing his name before the public, differs from it in this respect, that the latter one has been productive of great good in exposing the enormous amount of ignorance that prevails on the subject of swimming. Our readers will recollect that rather more than a year ago the public were startled by hearing that J. B. Johnson had dived off London Bridge and rescued from drowning an elderly gentleman named Mr. Peters, who had fallen off a steamboat. The gilt, however, was considerably removed from the gingerbread when it was afterwards discovered that the whole thing had been planned, and that old Mr. Peters was none other than Peter Johnson, J. B.'s brother, himself a very fine swimmer, who came in third when H. Gurr won the championship of the Thames, and who now calls himself the champion diver. However, the object was attained, Johnson's name was in every paper, and to this day he calls himself the " Hero of London Bridge." Bearing these facts in mind, we hope we shall not hurt the hero's feelings when we say that on the announcement that he was about to swim across the Channel we smelt a rat. How about the steamer to accompany the race? Suppose, owing to shallow water, or some other reason, the steamer would be obliged to leave him for a time alone with Mr. Peters in the small boat, and rejoin him afterwards in deeper water. Seeing is believing; we too had a small boat, and we can now inform Mr. Peter Johnson, in answer to the question addressed to his brother while swimming last Saturday, that the small boy in the boat was our small boy, and that we were ourselves following in a lugger, in company with a tin of Australian meat, a gallon of beer, and a bottle of sherry.

These precautions were, however, entirely unnecessary, by a circumstance occurring which we certainly did not anticipate. After swimming fairly (with the exception of three minutes, when he had hold of the tow-rope, the consequent increased pace he then progressed causing our boatman to take his jersey off in order to be able to row hard enough to keep up with him) for a little over an hour, the hero's legs failed him, and getting on board the steamer, he ended this feat, begun with such ceremony, by steaming away to Calais. Personally we were not sorry; the sea was lumpy, and our Australian meat, our beer, and our sherry would have fed the fishes had the hero's legs been much stronger.

The distance accomplished when he gave up is of course a matter of opinion, and everyone knows how difficult it is to judge distances at sea. It has been put down at about seven miles, but we do not think it was so much. However, this is merely a question of the strength of the tide, which runs exceedingly fast off Dover pier—so fast, indeed, off the pier-head, that a man cannot row a boat round close in against the stream. A black bottle sunk to about an inch from the cork thrown from the pier would reach off Folkestone in about an hour and a half, more or less, according to the wind. Supposing Johnson swam at the rate of two miles an hour or a little under, with the stream, he would go about six in the time in which he swam. It is ludicrous in the extreme to read the grave and learned opinions on the subject in some of the daily papers. For instance, the *Daily Telegraph* says: "We do not think it possible to swim in still water more than eight miles in two hours or four miles in one hour." Fancy Mr. Hotspur gravely stating that he did not think a three-year-old could run the

Derby course in less than 1 minute 21 seconds, when the whole world knows that it has never been done under 2 minutes 43 seconds. The *Standard*, however, out-Herods Herod, and after a manner apologises for only seven miles in the hour, on the ground that it was *against* a strong stream. We suppose, were these writers to go to a running match, they would account for a man's not running more than one mile in half-a-minute, on the ground that it was up-hill and against a strong wind. But how about those hard things "facts"? The Serpentine is 980 yards long from the railings to the bridge; it has been swum over and over again by first-rate men—Harry Gurr, Pamplin, Coulter, Tom Morris, Parker,. and others. *It has never yet been swum at the rate of one mile in half-an-hour.* The quickest time on record (we quote from memory) was done by Morris, who swam it in 16 minutes 45 seconds. It must be borne in mind, too, that this is only 100 yards over half-a-mile, and that a man can of course swim half-a-mile in *less* than half the time in which he could swim one mile, exactly as a man can run or walk half-a-mile in less than half the time he can run or walk one mile. J. B. Johnson may or may not be better than all these men, but we consider it impossible that he can be so much better than them—that he can swim a mile in twenty-six minutes; and consequently still think that the course at Hendon Lake was (accidentally of course) not measured correctly when he swam. Were he now to swim a length of the Serpentine in sixteen minutes it would, in our opinion, be a better proof of his being the best swimmer that has ever been known than anything he has yet done; that he could do it in the time in which it is said he did the first 1,000 yards at Hendon, we consider simply absurd and impossible. We do not wish to be hard upon Mr. Johnson, or to detract from his merits as a swimmer; on the contrary, we believe him to be undoubtedly the fastest swimmer in the country, and thank him for having brought swimming forward before the public in a way unprecedented; but on behalf of the public we consider it our duty to protest against the mass of absurdities that have lately appeared in some of the daily papers.

A certain amount of consideration is due to other professionals, and Mr. Johnson's attitude towards them is that of "Everyone for himself, as the elephant said to the chickens." With regard to what we believe to be the impossible feat of swimming across the Channel, the greatest difficulty to contend against is the cold. One of the hardiest swimmers we have ever known in this respect was Harry Gurr. When he won the championship of the Thames late in the autumn, the water was exceedingly cold; Gurr, however, came out as if nothing had happened, dressed himself in the boat, and helped to bring-to David Pamplin, who came in second, but who immediately became insensible from the effects of the cold. On one occasion, at Plymouth, Gurr remained in the sea five hours without touching boat or land, and without taking any refreshment.

If the Straits feat is *ever* accomplished, it will be done by a man of this description, but unless J. B. Johnson was in an exceptional state of health it would be worse than useless for him to attempt the feat again. To be seized with a cold after one hour's swim betrays a state of health resembling that of Heenan at the time of his encounter with Tom King—immense muscular development, but no vital power; what we want for it is a constitution resembling that of Tom Sayers.—*Land and Water,* August 31st, 1872.

GREAT SWIMMING RACE BETWEEN W. BECKWITH AND MORRIS, FOR £50.

GOOD genuine swimming races, like angels' visits, are few and far between, nor are swimmers to be blamed for such being the case. The pace at which it is possible to swim is so slow compared to the pace at which it is possible to run or at which horses can gallop, that just as the latter sport owes much of its popularity to its glorious uncertainty, so swimming races are unpopular owing to the fact of the respective merits of the principal professionals being so well known that few contests are really possible, except for prizes the result of which is generally a foregone conclusion. As instances in point, there have been this year already two races for the championship, the prize being on each occasion a 50-guinea cup. The attitude of the public has been that of the ring in a race where some good horse has started with the odds of 10 to 1 offered on him with no takers, viz., that of indifference. J. B. Johnson, the present champion, is so good a swimmer, that the result of each race was known to a certainty beforehand, and consequently it ceased to be a race at all.

It is only when some rising young swimmer just emerging from boyhood—which is, in our opinion, in swimming, the very prime of life—challenges some old and accomplished professional, that any real excitement becomes possible, and it is because such occasions are so rare that when they do occur the interest becomes so great. It was at the age of sixteen that David Pamplin won the 20-guinea cup, presented by a now defunct sporting paper, against all comers, one mile in the Thames, beating Donovan and all the best swimmers of the day. It was at sixteen, that Harry Gurr won the championship of England in such splendid style, that during the next three years no one had the courage to attempt to wrest it from him. Again, it is at the age of sixteen that Little Willie Beckwith —as he is still called—amidst the wildest excitement, in a bath thronged almost to suffocation, so nearly beat Tom Morris, the ex-champion of England, one of the finest of the many fine swimmers of the day.

The backers of each party seemed very confident. On the part of Morris, they knew that but a few years back he was the fastest swimmer in England, and though lately he has had to succumb to both Johnson and Parker, yet there was but little difference between him and the latter, and neither David Pamplin nor Coulter had a chance with him in a race in the Thames, which he swam soon after winning the amateur championship. Young Beckwith wants twenty-five seconds start of Parker, with whom Morris has lately trained, and in the opinion of many he was not only up to, but far better than his old form of three years back, by which in all probability he was judged by Beckwith. On the other hand, the friends of young Beckwith knew that his father was backing him, and that he is, perhaps, the best judge of swimming living. Was it likely that on the first occasion on which his boy swam a really important race, he would make so great a mistake as to underrate the powers of his opponent, an old and well-known swimmer? As to public performances, young Beckwith has but little to boast of, beyond invariably beating everyone of his own age with whom he has come in contact; for we consider his winning a cup at the Wenlock Baths, known as Tom Senn's Handicap, nothing, as owing to the extraordinary handicapping, the result could not have been otherwise had he been a far inferior swimmer to what he is. In the handicap in question, the present man, who now swims him a level 500 yards, was made to give him over a minute in 400 yards, and notwithstanding that " Boy Champion" was attached to his name, another little boy, J. Balding, younger than himself, who had never even won a prize, was absolutely handicapped to give him a start. However, this absurdity, or "eccentricity of genius," whichever it was, was not the fault of the boy, who was known by everyone

who knew anything at all about it to be one of the
fastest swimmers of the day. His father, Professor
Beckwith, too, was well known to be able to bring
his son up to the post in the best of condition—not
an easy thing always at an age when too often one
has to contend with the double difficulty of a pipe in
one pocket and an apple in the other. The result of
the race proves that W. Beckwith, though he did
not win, is nevertheless the fastest swimmer for his
age that has ever been known. But a few years back
to swim twelve lengths of the Lambeth Baths in
eight minutes was considered a wonderful performance; yet the loser last night did it under seven
minutes and a half. It is a strong argument against
the retrogression of the human race, that in all
athletic sports, the men of the present age are
superior to any that have gone before.

Shortly before starting, slight odds were laid on
Morris, but the betting gradually veered round with
even money offered on Beckwith, with no takers.
At twenty minutes to ten a capital start was
effected, and in the first length of the bath both
kept nearly level, but Morris gained about a yard on
completing the second. The first four lengths were
swum in two minutes ten seconds by Morris, he
being about two yards ahead of his young opponent,
and gradually increasing his lead he ultimately won
by about ten yards, in the extraordinary time of
seven minutes seventeen seconds, the fastest time

on record in which twelve lengths of the Lambeth
Baths have ever been swum. W. Beckwith's time
was seven minutes twenty-seven and a half seconds.

The boy, however, though he has lost the race,
has more than maintained his honour. He has done
that which no one of his age has ever done before.
Gurr and Pamplin in their day never swam as he
did. Morris, in fact, suprised every one in beating
all his former performances, and it was said by many
good judges that his trainer, Parker, has taught him
even to beat himself. Of course popular feeling was
in favour of the boy, just as in a street-fight the
most disinterested looker-on is sure to say "Go it,
little'un."

Young Beckwith must console himself with the
thought that if at sixteen—and he only attained that
age last month—he can swim as he now does, he will
before long, by the exercise of patience, practice and
self-denial, make for himself not only a greater name
than his father has, but prove himself superior to any
swimmer that has ever yet appeared.—*Standard*,
September 30th, 1873.

HARRY PARKER AT THE CITY OF LONDON BATHS.

MANY attempts have been and are being made to raise the lowest strata of the London poor to a higher level. Perhaps none of these attempts are more worthy of notice than the efforts made to instil into their minds a love of cleanliness. Certain, however, is it that the London swimming baths are the means of bringing water in contact with hundreds of thousands of lads who would otherwise swell the ranks of the great unwashed.

There is no human being so low that does not possess some quality by which he may be raised, if it be rightly treated. It has been suggested that the elevation of the negro race may be accomplished by acting on their ruling passion of the love of finery. However that may be, the love of sport, inherent in all Englishmen, is a strong motive power among the lower classes. In what some still call the good old times, when prizefighters were honest, the bull-dog-visaged rough would risk six months' hard labour to witness one of the old-fashioned encounters, and it is doubtful if the whole of Aldershot camp would be sufficient to enforce a

charge for admission to Epsom Downs on the
Derby Day similar to the Course at Paris.   As an
instance of how much races are the cause of lads
learning to swim, we would mention the fact that
since the Regatta Committee at Ryde, in the Isle of
Wight, have instituted two races for boys under 16,
in which in each the first prize was £1, second 15s.,
third 10s., and fourth 5s., there is scarcely a boy in
Ryde that does not know how to swim.   It is much
to be regretted that such large sums of money should
be annually spent in promoting a sport in which the
welfare of horses is somewhat neutralised by the
degradation of human beings connected with them,
while no encouragement whatever is given to a sport
like swimming, which is inseparable from cleanliness,
and is the means of saving annually hundreds of
human lives.   The Registrar-General reports that
the average loss of life each year from drowning in
England and Wales alone amounts to the awful
total of 2608.   Were a sum of money such as £200
annually granted, to be given away in prizes, say one
mile in the Serpentine, first man, £100; second, £50;
third, £20; fourth, £10; and £5 for each of the next
four, probably such an impetus would be given to
swimming that this total would soon show considerable decrease.   At present, perhaps, nobody has done
more to lessen it than the London Swimming Club,
and it was under the auspices of this club that
Harry Parker, the champion swimmer of London,

last night took his complimentary benefit at Golden Lane. Golden Lane certainly does not remind one of the Golden Age. A long narrow thoroughfare, filthy and dirty, where at night the police walk in couples, intersected with courts still more filthy and dirty, where they dare not walk at all. Golden Lane, with its 4d. lodging houses and thriving gin palaces, has at least one redeeming spot, a sort of oasis in a desert of dirt, the City of London Baths appeal to the passers by to wash and be clean. The amount of good done by this bath to the neighbourhood in which it is placed is incalculable. Many a ragged lad has taken his first step in civilisation—a paper collar on Sunday, owing to the sleek appearance his washed face and wet combed hair have given him when, on leaving the bath, he has caught a glimpse of himself reflected in a shop window. The principal feature in the programme for last night's entertainment was the *début* of Parker's little sister, Emily Parker, aged 11: the gracefulness and ease with which the child swam about the bath and floated on her back, proves at any rate that swimming can be easily acquired by the other sex. As, however, at present the most advanced advocates of women's rights have not made it a grievance that half the navy is not womened, instead of manned, perhaps it is not so important that swimming should become popular among ladies. We fear that nothing short of a race in the Serpentine between two duchesses, for

F

1000 pairs of white kid gloves a side, will ever make it
fashionable. That there are, however, occasions
when swimming is necessary for women as well as men
was never better proved than last night. Harry Parker
is deservedly popular, and his name alone is sufficient
to fill any bath when it has been announced that he
will appear. The City of London Baths were
consequently crowded almost to suffocation, when,
on the appearance of the little girl, a cry arose, "Room
for the ladies," as some dozen or more attempted to
obtain a view of the wonderful performance of by far
the best "girl" that ever yet entered the water in
public. The welcome the ladies received was truly
English. Room was made by strong muscular arms
where apparently no room a moment before was
possible. Unfortunate, however, was the result.
After a short period, during which the thronged bath
went almost beside itself in applauding a child's first
efforts—crash—part of the flooring, raised about five
feet over the deepest part of the bath, gave way,
and in one instant at least fifty persons, including
some of the above-named ladies, were struggling in
six feet of water. An accident, however, in the
water at a swimming entertainment is somewhat
akin to a man being seized with a fit at a meeting of
the medical society—the danger is in the multitude
of help. In almost a second of time dozens of good
swimmers had plunged in, foremost among whom we
noticed David Pamplin, who brought safely, not to

shore, but into his depth a youth who, evidently unable to swim, had been clinging with a face white with terror to an iron rod just within his reach. Pamplin then with great presence of mind dived backwards and forwards under the *débris* of floating planks and excited bathers in a manner which precluded the possibility of even "one old gentleman being missing," as after old Mr. Weller's famous stage-coach accident. In the excitement of the moment a suit of real clothes, not a suit picked for the purpose, seemed no hindrance, and no exhibition race could prove how important this feature is in swimming entertainments. It is, in fact, swimming brought into its practical relations as regards saving human life. Fortunately, no harm has been done save some possible colds that may have been caught on the occasion; and of course Parker cannot be blamed for the insecurity of the bath flooring, which, we regret to state we were informed, gave way in a somewhat similar manner about two years ago.

The races, none of which were concluded, will be finished on Monday next at the same baths, when it is to be hoped some competent surveyor will report that all is right before the crush of persons that were assembled last night, and through whom it was almost impossible to elbow a way, are allowed to reassemble. We would suggest, too, that some space should be set apart for members of the press, many of whom were present. That Parker's sister

is destined to become a great attraction there can be
no doubt; perhaps nothing speaks better for his
powers as a teacher than that at the end of two
months' instruction this little girl swims well enough
to beat most boys of sixteen who enter for races.   It
is to be hoped that Parker will be rewarded for his
long exertions as the almost "honorary swimming
master" to the London Swimming Club by a good
appointment at a bath in a neighbourhood where the
friendly caution of a policeman—a swarm of whom
had quickly assembled outside after the accident—
"You had better take care how you walk down, sir,"
will be unnecessary.   All praise, however, is due to
the London Swimming Club in choosing a locality
where their efforts are really valuable in encouraging
cleanliness, for "those that are whole need not a
physician."—*Standard*, October 7th, 1873.

CAPTAIN WEBB'S FIRST SWIM ACROSS THE CHANNEL.

THE first attempt made by Captain Webb to swim across the Channel took place on Thursday, August 12th; and there can be no doubt, on calmly looking back upon the circumstances under which this first attempt was made, that the start was a foolish one. Much excuse, however, must be made for Captain Webb, we think, for starting as he did, all things being considered. I had been waiting in company with a good many other gentlemen connected with the London press at Dover ever since Monday morning; and, now that his great attempt has been crowned with success, no one would think our time and trouble were thrown away. Still, it must be borne in mind that the universal impression among us, one and all, was that we were engaged in what may be termed "a wild-goose chase." Fabulous odds were offered against the attempt being successful, and no takers for these odds could be found. Considerable pressure was put upon Webb too, at any rate, if possible, not to let so many connected with the press, who came a long distance purposely to witness his performance, return to London without some effort on his part to show that he was at least worthy of the attentions he had received. Upon Thursday morning, therefore, the sea being fairly calm, it was with considerable pleasure that we were informed that the long looked-for moment had arrived, and that, in a few hours' time, Captain Webb would be breasting the waves. Telegrams were dispatched announcing positively that the start would take place. The lugger by which he was accompanied was got into water and provisioned for the journey. Besides the lugger, two small boats were engaged to accompany him, one of which contained the umpire and Webb's personal attendant, Mr. Ward, his cousin; the other acting as a sort of dispatch-boat to and fro between the other little boat and the lugger. Unfortunately, a few hours before the start actually occurred, a thunderstorm had taken place; and the sea, which up to this moment, had been smooth and calm, was now decidedly lumpy. Looking back dispassionately upon what then occurred, Captain Webb was somewhat to be pitied. He was placed on the horns of a dilemma. On the one hand he felt that to succeed, should the sea continue as it then was, was next door to impossible. On the other hand, had he given up his attempt, and should he at any future time announce his intention to start, such intention would possibly be looked upon as the boy's cry of "Wolf, wolf!" Start therefore he did, trusting to the sea gradually calming down, and of this there seemed to be some chance. The owner of the lugger was a Mr. Toms, of the " Shakspeare Inn," Dover, one of the most experienced pilots in the neighbour-hood, and a cool-headed, quiet, sober, thinking man, whose gray hair and keen eye in themselves inspired confidence. The crew consisted of six sailors well accustomed to combat the Channel waves, and two of them were Mr. Toms' own sons. Speaking for myself, it was with a feeling of profound emotion that I watched the man, ready prepared for his voyage, walk calmly down the Admiralty Pier, with a rug thrown over his shoulders, prepared to start. There was a look of bold determination in his eye, yet tinged with sadness, which bespoke the inner consciousness of the impossibility of what he was about to attempt. The end of the pier was reached; and, after a short delay, Webb, throwing the rug from off his shoulders, plunged in. During his stand on the buttress at the end of the pier, a few feet above the level of the water, there was a look in his face that seemed to say: " I have cast my life on a single throw of the die." With one good look-out to sea, much such as Ham Peggoty might have given when he put forth to reach the wreck, to attempt to save the life of one who turned out to be the destroyer of his life's happiness—one such look, and he plunged into the water. A ringing cheer went up from the crowd assembled on the pier.

During the next hour Webb contended bravely with
the rolling billows, while the majority of those on
board the lugger vainly contended against the awful
pangs of sea-sickness. We had on board one or two
artists; but oh! for the magic pencil of a Leech, to
have handed down to posterity the sketch that might
have been made of "our own correspondents at
sea!" There is, perhaps, no greater leveller than
a rough sea. Dignity is incompatible with retching.
Fortunately, for my part, I can say, like the very
old turkey in "Pickwick," when he overheard his
master propose killing him for the London market,
"I am pretty tough, and that is one consolation."

But I must not be led away from my subject by
the remembrance of our own trials and sufferings, but
return to the bold man in the water. And here let
me remark that I am not at all sure but what the
first performance of Captain Webb, though it was
unsuccessful, was not in reality a greater one than
that of his last successful one. On starting there
was but little tide running. What little tide there
was ran eastward, and by half-past six o'clock
Webb, who had swam a mile and a half from shore,
had been carried by it in a line off Dover Castle.
After this point the tide began to run considerably
stronger, and by a little after seven o'clock we
were in a line with the coast-guard station, about
half way between Dover and a very pleasant little
spot known as St. Margaret's Bay. The little

rowing boat that kept close to watch was, of course, provided with a good compass, and it never got further than six or seven yards away from the swimmer. Unfortunately, owing to the state of the sea, it was almost impossible for the lugger to keep close to the little boat. Accordingly some natural anxiety was felt, not only by the two in the little boat, but by those on board the lugger, lest by any possible chance we might lose sight of one another. By half-past seven the sun went down with a somewhat angry look. Now this period of sunset had been looked forward to by those most competent to give an opinion as the time most likely for the sea to quiet. Of course, owing to the lugger not being able to be under sail except to an extremely trifling amount, in order to keep with the little boat, the rolling movement was precisely similar to what it would have been had she been anchored. The rolling was something fearful, and most on board were far too prostrate to watch the swimmer. Fortunately, however, the sea began somewhat to abate, which seemed to encourage Webb, who at this period asked for something to eat. He was supplied with a little underdone cold meat, and seemed to gain courage from the refreshment which he took and the better prospect that the abating sea afforded him. There was, at present, no difficulty whatever in steering. The double bright lights of the South Foreland were distinctly visible, as well as the South Sand Head light, which is situated at the extreme south end of the Goodwin Sands. Cape Grisnez light, on the opposite coast, could also be seen with the naked eye, whilst Calais light could be seen with a good glass. Though the sea was rough the evening was particularly clear, and the long line of lights, both at Dover and Deal, twinkled in the distance like a bright tiara of diamonds set in blue enamel. At half-past eight Webb seemed very confident. He was swimming very strongly, had no sensation of cold, and evidently seemed more confident than he did at starting, owing to the sea having very much abated. At nine o'clock we were in a line with the South Sand Head light and Deal. The lugger was still rolling frightfully, and what notes I took at the time, for which my present account is indebted, were scribbled with the stump end of a lead pencil on damp paper by the light of a tallow candle, amidst prostrate and groaning men. Webb had now gone seven miles on his road—not simply seven miles with the stream, but he had advanced absolutely seven miles nearer the French coast than when he started; and we informed him, much to his delight, that he had swam at more than the rate he had anticipated, namely, one mile and a half in the hour. The opinion on board the lugger was that he had a very good chance of being successful. A 9.30 we heard the gun at Dover boom through the distance and took advantage of it to

compare our watches. Up to this time the sea had
been getting better and better. At a little after ten,
however, a sudden shifting wind occurred, and down
came the rain in such volumes as would have suggested to a Yankee mind the possibility of "swimming up it " into the lugger, had he felt so disposed.
The little boat and the lugger for some time entirely
lost sight of one another—our only communication
being that the little boat burned at intervals blue
lights, while we responded on board the lugger
with what sailors call a " flamer." This primitive
but effective sea-signal consists of dipping a stick
of wood, round the end of which has been rolled a
piece of tow, into a bottle of turpentine, setting fire
to the tow and holding it aloft in the air. The only
shelter that I could obtain on board the lugger was
a little close and stuffy cabin, the temperature of
which resembled the inner room of a Turkish bath,
into which little furnace I had to take occasional
plunges in order to scribble down a few facts that
would enable me to give a faithful account of one of
the finest and pluckiest efforts I have ever witnessed
in my life, and which, as I have before said, in my
opinion even surpassed the successful attempt on the
24th. A little after eleven, in answer to a signal from
the little boat, our dispatch-boat took out a supply
of fresh candles to supply the lantern which hung
at the bow of Webb's own boat. The weather,
however, looked very threatening, and the sea was

rising every minute. Those of us who were not ill
had succeeded in making a substantial but rather
rough-and-tumble supper from out of the hamper
that had been very kindly supplied by Mr. Fry,
proprietor of the " Harp Hotel," Dover. At this
period we must have been fully nine miles from
shore, and I put forth in this little boat to consult
with Webb on the advisability of his remaining
longer in the water ; as, should the sea continue to
rise much more, it would almost have been impossible for a little boat to have lived. At the same
time it was equally impossible for us to leave a man
alone in mid-Channel with nothing but his pluck
and muscles to withstand the waves. One could not
but notice the deep tone of disappointment that
could be detected in his still strong and hearty
voice. In a dark night, with a rolling sea, which
would have deterred tens of thousands of his country-
men from attempting to cross even in a well fitted
mail-service boat, he had, by sheer strength and determination, accomplished more than half the distance.
But to contend against a sea that was now rolling
would have been simply the act of a madman. At a
quarter before midnight Captain Webb called out to
his cousin, in a tone which I shall never forget, so
tinged was it with despair : " Its of no use con-
tinuing. There is too much sea on." A few minutes
afterwards he caught hold of the small boat's side,
jumped into it with far greater ease than the majority

of bathers after a ten minutes' dip, and was quickly rowed alongside the lugger. He quickly rubbed himself down and, throwing on a few clothes, paced impatiently the rolling deck, and giving us unfortunate landsmen a lesson on the utility of having sea-legs. Captain Webb is a sailor to the backbone, and there are few men living under whom I would rather sail. He quietly said: " It would have been of no use; that little boat would not have lived above a quarter of an hour, so I shall turn in." Turn in he did into the Turkish bath in question, which to this day, I fancy, must smell of porpoise oil. A short consultation was now held on board as to what was to be done next. On this point, fortunately, there was no dissenting voice. With one accord we all agreed—run to the nearest port, which proved to be Calais. Webb slept calmly for another four hours, while we tossed through the now raging sea until the welcome harbour came in view in early daylight. Captain Webb seemed none the worse for his exertions, and, fortunately, he had proved himself so great a swimmer that he was no loser by his want of success. The editor of *Land and Water* very kindly volunteered to receive any sums that might be collected on his behalf to assist him to attempt it again on a more favourable opportunity. Mr. Chinnery, of the Stock Exchange, also kindly made a collection ; and, in a very short time, Webb was placed in a position in which he could "bide his time" without difficulty. Considering that Captain Webb had remained in the water for nearly seven hours, and left as fresh and as strong, and as free from any effect of cold, as when he entered it, no doubt could remain on any impartial mind that, at any rate, under favourable circumstances the feat was not impossible. It was this preconceived notion of its being impossible that had been taken up by many persons, whose strength of opinion is too often proportionate to their ignorance of the subject, that had a great detracting effect upon his efforts. Naturally Webb's one thought was, considering the *fiascos* of one or two who had gone before him, that when he did attempt to swim the Channel, to make sure of being accompanied by a sufficient number of well-known respectable witnesses, who could put the truth of what he had done beyond even the possibility of doubt. In this he succeeded, and the bitterness of disappointment which he naturally felt must have been considerably alleviated by the feeling that, should he again try, at all events he would not be alone. Webb, therefore, quietly returned to Dover, with a determination that, though foiled once, he would try and try again till success might form a wreath to surround his brow.

WEBB'S SUCCESSFUL SWIM ACROSS THE CHANNEL.

A MORE beautiful morning than that of the
24th August last could not be conceived. No wind,
no waves, but little tide, and the sea presenting
that rarely calm appearance as if oil had been
poured upon the waters. Captain Webb may think
himself fortunate in having secured such a day for
his swim across the Channel, for there can be no
doubt that only under circumstances such as
these would success be possible. It had been
his original intention to start at one o'clock in the
morning; and many, myself among them—under the
impression that we were bound to make a night of
it—had, late on Monday evening, drunk strong coffee
to keep ourselves awake. Unfortunately, not only
for us, but for Captain Webb, the sea suddenly
changed, and the attempt had to be postponed.
After a somewhat restless night, I rose early on
Tuesday morning, and about eleven o'clock Captain
Webb informed me that he had determined to start
at once. The lugger was got ready in all haste, not
forgetting the provisions. As we had a small open
cooking stove on board, we took with us, in addition

to what we had taken before, a good-sized piece of bacon, a basket of eggs, and a frying-pan. At four minutes before one o'clock, Captain Webb, well smothered in porpoise grease, dived in from the end of the Admiralty Pier. The start had taken place so unexpectedly that there was by no means a crowd present such as would probably have collected had it been known earlier. It was a beautiful, bright, sunshiny day; and as he swam away from the pier, his broad shoulders shooting through the water, and gleaming in the light of the sun, he very much resembled some large seal or huge fish, not merely in smell, but in appearance. Of course, under such circumstances, anything like sea-sickness was out of the question, and a very merry party indeed we formed on board the lugger. I think there is an old saying, "that one month on board a ship, in way of friendship, is equal to a year on land." Considering how limited was our space, I think I may add that one day in an open boat is equal to a month on board a ship. However, I must not forget the brave man in the water who has been swimming bravely on since four minutes to one o'clock, and who, at starting, almost immediately began to feel the effect of the tide, which ran westward, that is, in the direction of Folkestone. He continued to drift in this direction for about two hours, but was not carried by it more than a mile and a half. As it afterwards turned out, it would have been far better if he had started two hours earlier. But then this is, of course, judging from consequences—a very illogical method of reasoning.

2 P.M.—We were still making way down Channel with the ebb, which at its full force runs one and a half knots an hour; but on the slack water that takes place between the times of the ebb and flow we made less progress down Channel, but farther distance from the land. It was a hazy afternoon, but not much glare; nor was there any ripple on the water which would have necessitated the gauze-spectacles then. So far, everything tended to a successful end. Several small boats that had come from land to look at us began now gradually to drop off one by one, though one light skiff, containing two personal friends of my own, stuck closely with us; and, indeed, they announced their intention of coming the whole way across, which, however, was afterwards abandoned. A large keg of beer on board the lugger was viewed by them with wistful eyes, but we economised our provisions, promising a glass of beer each in payment for their carrying back dispatches.

2.45 P.M.—We could see the mail packet coming across, and the crowd on the deck nearest to us proved that we had been seen, which was afterwards confirmed by a faint cheer heard in the distance. Webb had started swimming with a stroke of twenty-two to the minute, and varied from this to twenty-one. At the

G

end of his swim this was reduced to eighteen strokes a minute. It has been erroneously stated that Webb, during part of the time, swam at the rate of twenty-six strokes a minute. This, however, would be impossible. A fast breast-stroke swimmer like Coulter, the late great Serpentine swimmer, could, perhaps, keep this up for a mile; but to maintain such a speed for five or even ten hours would be as impossible as to run a mile at the same rate as a man can run a hundred yards.

3 P.M.—Quantities of porpoises were now dancing around us, some could be seen close to the swimmer. It was even thought seriously by some that these creatures may have been attracted by the smell of their grease with which Webb had anointed himself; and, of course, various jokes were made with reference to catching some of them. It was also said that, perhaps, after all, it was a Barnum affair, and that Webb had bribed some of the porpoises to shove him along. Soon after this a small rowing boat, which had put out from Dover, came alongside; but, unfortunately, we were not able to take on board the gentleman who had come out for that purpose. However, it afterwards proved that the gentleman in question was a medical man, a surgeon-major attached to the garrison of Dover; and we deeply regretted that we did not know the fact at the time, as he, of all others, was the man we should have most liked to have had with us. One

of the perils against which Webb had to be upon his guard was the jelly fish. It may not be generally known that these apparently innocent-looking animals—or vegetables, whatever they are —have it in their power to inflict a very painful sting. On one occasion when Webb had been prac-tising, previous to his swim to Ramsgate, he came dead against one of these large, yellow jelly fish, or water-starches as the sailors call them. The effect was very serious, as he had immediately to get out of the water, and in a few minutes was very sick. However, the one in question must have been an unusually large one. Some of these water-starches are blue in appearance, and are quite as dangerous, if not more so, than the yellow ones. The white ones, however, appear to be innocuous.

3.30 P.M.—The tide now began to turn. Captain Webb had, however, drifted but very little to the west. Had he, at this period of the turn of the tide, been somewhere off Folkestone, he would pro-bably have saved some four or five hours at the finish, and the importance of this will be seer further on. Webb had, notwithstanding, made very great use of his time, and was fully four miles from shore.

4 P.M.—The weather now began to grow some-what hazy, and Dover Castle stood forth in misty relief in the distance; but few sounds disturbed the scene, save the monotonous movement of the heavy

oars, which creaked backwards and forwards in
regular time like huge pendulums. The sea literally
swarmed with fish, and shoal after shoal would
occasionally dash by within fifty yards of the lugger,
being pursued probably by some porpoises, which
still continued to bob up and down all around us.
About this period Webb took his first refreshment,
which simply consisted of some good, strong beef tea.
Another hour passed by, and still the sea retained its
glassy surface. Occasionally a sound would be heard
at a distance, somewhat resembling that of persons
taking in coals a few doors off, and for some time I
was extremely puzzled to know what this sound
possibly could be. Mr. Toms, our pilot, however,
informed me, with a smile at my ignorance, that it
was some ship laying out at anchor, and the sound
I heard was that of the heavy anchor chain falling
downwards. Webb was still swimming strongly and
cheerfully onward, occasionally conversing with those
in the little boat, which, of course, kept close to
him as well as the lugger, which, owing to there
being no wind, had no difficulty in so doing. All on
board were in excellent spirits, and young Baker,
who combines a very good knowledge of cooking in
addition to his diving powers, was commissioned to
get the tea ready. About six o'clock we espied in the
distance a small black spot on the water, which
seemed to increase in size rather than otherwise.
By the help of a good glass we made out that it was

a small rowing boat, and it was evidently approaching
us. As it gradually neared, a practised eye could
well detect that the movement of at least one of
the oars was that of a first-class oarsman. As it
gradually came closer to us, the face of an extremely
muscular friend, whose gigantic muscles have often
led him to victory on the River Cam some fifteen
years ago, came prominently into view. It was
somewhat amusing to watch the face of the waterman who had accompanied him, who was puffing
and blowing, and seemed as if he had had enough of
it already. However, go back he must, and he
looked it. Mr. "Muscles," however, had not turned
a hair, refusing either beer or spirits which we offered
him, taking, instead, a deep draught of tea, and ate also
a few slices of bread and butter, refusing a nice rich
omelette which had just been turned out of the frying-
pan by Mr. Baker's skilful hands. Mr. " Muscles"
stripped and swam by Webb's side for five or ten
minutes, and, indeed, in breadth of beam between
the two there was not much to choose. Not a hand-
some cab in London could have taken in the two
abreast. Mr. "Muscles," however, left the water, dried
himself, and started on his homeward journey,
refusing foolishly the offer of a pocket compass, as
if any mist had arisen on the road back, or had the
sea suddenly become rough, they would probably
both have been drowned. However, they succeeded
in getting close to the South Sand Head light, and

then rowed into Dover along the shore; the poor
waterman being far too much exhausted, and probably too much in awe of Mr. "Muscles'" muscles to
dispute about his fare. We were informed, a few days
afterwards, that nothing in this world would ever
induce him to enter a boat again with that gentleman. Soon after seven o'clock the sun set, throwing
a golden ray of glory over the glassy surface of the
sea, and lighting up the full-set sails of two or
three large vessels vainly endeavouring to catch a
breeze, not far from us, with that peculiar rosy-
coloured glow rarely witnessed save in a sunset
on the Alps. We were many of us now becoming
drowsy. The previous bad night's rest which we had
had, owing to the coffee which we had taken, began
to tell; and there is something in a perfectly smooth
sea and the monotonous sound of the oars that
seems to invite slumber. However, a slight repast
being proposed, we all became instantly awake, and
(thanks to Mr. Fry's—of the Harp Hotel, Dover—
well-stocked hamper) cold chicken, cold meat and
salad, quickly began to disappear. All this time
Webb continued swimming with the same steady
stroke—about twenty to the minute. He rarely
spoke. He evidently determined to do or die. It
now began to grow dark, and, as the moon had not
yet risen, we witnessed that splendid and somewhat
rare sight, a phosphorescent sea. As the heavy oars
dipped in the water they seemed to throw off in

every direction millions of bright gems, by the side
of which even diamonds would have looked lustre-
less. As Webb ploughed through the water, each
long and steady stroke surrounded him with a halo of
glory, owing to the phosphorescent state of the sea,
which resembled those depicted in the engravings
we often see of the early Christian martyrs.

9 P.M.—Webb still continued swimming well on,
and hitherto had made no complaint. He had now
been in the water eight hours, and seemed as strong
as ever, when he suddenly cried out, " I am stung."
It startled all of us; for knowing what had happened
on the previous occasion, we felt this very probably
might be the signal for giving up the attempt.
Fortunately, however, the jelly-fish in question had
only touched his shoulder. We quickly took him a
little brandy, and in a few minutes he reported
himself as feeling all right. I may add that previous
to this he had taken some coffee, but no solid food.
About ten o'clock a small tug, that had come out
from Dover for the purpose, came close to us, and
one or two in a little boat put out, and came close
by Webb. They were very uncommunicative, and
refused to take back any dispatches. They stayed
but a short time, and then left us.

11.45 P.M.—We at length sighted the Calais
mail-boat, the paddle-wheels of which we had
distinctly heard in the distance for nearly three-
quarters of an hour. The steamer comes within a

hundred yards of us, and a good, hearty, ringing cheer goes up. We burn a red light, which casts a ruddy glow over the whole scene, and lights up Webb's face so that he can distinctly be seen from the mail-boat. It was a curious sight, the red light showing up the flapping sails of the lugger and the two little rowing boats on the perfectly smooth sea. The mail-boat, however, passes on, and we are again left alone, the cheers dying away in the distance.

12 P.M.—The moon had by this time risen and the sky was clear, so that Webb could be distinctly seen from the lugger. According to the opinion of those on board the mail whom we saw afterwards, we must at this period have been about thirteen miles from Dover.

1 A.M.—Still the same steady swim, with no request for refreshment. Webb going like a well-balanced clock, doing nearly twenty strokes per minute.

2 A.M.—For the last two hours nothing very particular had occurred, We were drifting westward, and the white chalk cliffs near Cape Grisnez, lit up by the moon, were distinctly visible, as well, of course, as the revolving light, which appeared quite close by and high up out of the water. Webb himself could see the light from where he was swimming, and seemed cheered by the light.

2.10 A.M.—We were so near Cape Grisnez—about

three miles it was calculated—that there appeared to be every probability of success. Webb, who had now been over thirteen hours in the water, however, gave evident symptoms of fatigue, and young Baker stripped, and with the belt round his chest and life-line attached, got into the little boat, and sat by my side, ready for emergencies. It is but justice to the boy to add that he stuck to his post all through the night, till he plunged in and swam by Webb's side during the last mile.

3 A.M.—Webb now asked for a little beef-tea, which was promptly administered; he appeared very anxious, as he knew the tide would shortly turn; he was, however, now only swimming six-teen strokes to the minute, and appeared to labour very much.

3.45 A.M.—Old Toms had proved himself right about the tide, and had we started two hours earlier on the ebb, and thereby got some miles farther westward, all would have been right, and we should have touched Cape Grisnez in another hour. How-ever, Webb swam manfully on, but looked very queer and disappointed.

4 A.M.—Daylight had now appeared. Webb up to this point had taken some hot coffee, beef-tea, and cod-liver oil, but no solid food. He trod water while drinking, and refused to rest his hand on Mr. Ward's (his cousin's) arm, while taking it, though he was told to do so by the referee.

5 A.M.—It was now broad daylight, and the sun had risen; a haze, however, was over the land, and hid it from view. It was supposed by sunrise that we were within two and a half miles of Cape Grisnez, but, alas! the time had been somewhat miscalculated. Webb had thought he would have done the swim in about fourteen hours, but he had been in the water sixteen hours, and the tide turned and carried him every moment farther and farther away from the goal he so longed to reach.

6.30 A.M.—Webb still swimming on, but evidently much weaker. There seemed, too, some signs of wind springing up, and the sea, which up to this time had been a dead calm, now became rippled, and the short, little, chopping waves seemed to distress the swimmer very much. He began to lose all hope.

7.30 A.M.—Land still in sight but rather farther off than before; the tide seems running away from shore, Webb swimming fifteen strokes to the minute.

8 A.M.—Webb had some beef-tea followed by a sip of brandy, and Toms said that if he could hold out another three hours he might just reach Calais Pier.

9 A.M.—The wind had unfortunately very much increased, so much so indeed that it occasionally washed over the little boats in which we were seated. At this moment there was but one opinion,

and that was that he had no chance. The tide
sweeps round Cape Grisnez Point and bears away
from the shore.

10 A.M.—Webb, fearfully exhausted, still toiled on,
but was if anything farther from shore at ten o'clock
than he was at nine; his hands now began to drop
and fingers open, a bad sign, and he barely made
any way at all.

We had, however, during this hour drifted till we
were directly off Calais Pier. A boat belonging to
the Royal Mail Packet Service put off, and very useful indeed it was, as it got to windward of Webb, and
acted as a sort of breakwater. Webb was very weak,
and could barely do more than keep himself up; his
hands seemed to drop, and his legs were so weak
that he could barely bring them together at the end
of each stroke. By ten o'clock, however, the tide
had become slack, and by watching the head of the
pier we could see that at last Webb was drawing
slowly into shore.

Here Baker plunged in and swam by his side
through the waves, which were crested with what is
known as horses' heads. We sounded and found
that we were in five fathoms of water, and by 10.15
we could not have been more than 200 yards from
shore, but Webb was barely keeping afloat. It was
now or never—twelve strokes a minute, and scarcely
that.

10.20 A.M.—The excitement was intense; a crowd

had gathered on the sands near the pier ; the men in the mail-boat and lugger cheered till they were hoarse.

10.30 A.M.—It now became apparent that Webb would do it ; we were within 100 yards of shore; the men on the mail-boat struck up " Rule Britannia," and two of them stripped off their clothes to be ready to help directly Webb should touch land.

10.37 A.M.—Webb, whose face was incrusted with salt, sounded, but failed to touch land, and had some little difficulty in regaining his position. Mr. Ward, Webb's cousin, had taken off his coat and boots, but fortunately there was no occasion for him to plunge in. Webb's face was a strange mixture of red and white, and there was a deep red line across the back of his neck, from having kept his head back so long.

10.41 A.M.—A ringing shout. Webb, who feared to sound before, had touched ground in about three feet of water, and tries to stand up, but falls heavily forward. In a second the two men from the mail-boat are by his side, and each take his arm. They afterwards say he felt like a huge lump of cold tallow, from the grease. They assist him to shore, where an open trap is waiting, and Webb, rolled in a rug, is driven off to the Paris Hotel, Calais.

The men return to the mail-boat smelling horribly of porpoise grease. But tears of joy were in every eye. Not an eye on board the lugger but was full.

Poor old Toms cried like a child, the tears rolling down his honest weather-beaten countenance. However, we now made for the harbour, and pulled up alongside of the " Castalia," and made the best of our way to the hotel to which we had known Webb had been carried.

It took some time for our lugger to get round from the sands by the side of the pier into the harbour itself, and on our arriving at the hotel we found Webb comfortably rolled up in a thick blanket, and apparently asleep. He had partaken of some hot port wine and water, though, judging by my own experience of what French port wine is, I think it was about the worst thing in the world that could be given him. Webb slept comfortably for three hours, when he got up, dressed himself, and had some fish to eat, and after which he walked in the court-yard of the hotel and smoked a cigar, as if nothing had happened. The general opinion of the Calais people (I mean the natives) seems to have been that our lugger was a floating lunatic asylum, and that Webb himself was the biggest lunatic of the whole company. However, as the facts of the case began to dawn upon them, they began to regard Webb in the light of some extraordinary being, half man, half fish, and gratified their curiosity by pushing their way into his bed-room where he lay asleep, and exclaimed, with their shoulders on a level with their hats, " Ah! mon Dieu, mon Dieu!"

Webb went to bed on Wednesday night at ten o'clock, and slept very soundly until six o'clock in the morning, on which day he returned to Dover on board the "Castalia." And we here gladly embrace the opportunity of thanking the authorities of that splendid ship for the great courtesy displayed not only to himself, but to all of us. It is a trying task, having been in an open boat all night without one wink of sleep, and labouring under the excitement inseparable from having witnessed the greatest deed of athletics in any generation past or present, to bring one's self calmly down into a state of mind in which an accurate account could be written. However it had to be done and was done, but, considering the state of the sea, it would not have been possible for me to have written what I did on board any other vessel but the "Castalia" herself. Webb landed at Dover on Thursday afternoon at 3.30 p.m., and the first real ringing British cheer then broke on Webb's ears. For a cheer to be effective, it requires a multitude, and the crowd at the pier, notwithstanding that the great majority of the sporting population were away at Dover races, sent forth a shout that even shook the beams of the "Castalia" herself. Webb said he was only too glad to set foot on British soil again, though at the same time, with a smile, he honestly confessed that the most thrilling moment in his life was when he touched the French shore. And now I must close this eventful story, and leave my good friend Webb in an atmosphere of conquering hero, champagne and kindness, honestly trusting that he will not meet with his death by either of the last two named.

A. G. P.

MORE FACSIMILE REISSUES FROM PRYOR PUBLICATIONS

Old London Street Cries

'A beautiful pocket-sized facsimile, complete with *faux marbre* cover, lovely thick cream paper and cream ribbons to keep it shut . . . provides a brief history, an essay on cockney pronunciation and an index of street cries, in addition to the superb little engravings of street vendors and their cries.' *London Evening Standard.*

*First published 1885   156 pages   over 50 woodcuts
hardback   ISBN: 0 946014 00 0*   **£7.**95

Everybody's Book of Correct Conduct
Being the Etiquette of Everyday Life

'It is certain that he who lives correctly every day will find himself following the higher laws of morality and rectitude.'

*First published 1893   192 pages
ISBN: 0 946014 37 X   paperback*   **£4.**99

A SHORT HISTORY OF THE WOLF IN BRITAIN

Taken from James Harting's 'British Animals Extinct Within Modern Times', first published in 1880, here are early accounts of the wolf in the British Isles until its demise around 1760.   **£5.**95
96 pages   Illustrated   ISBN: 0 946014 27 2   Paperback

THE NATURAL HISTORY OF STUCK-UP PEOPLE

ALBERT SMITH

'We are about to expose, as simply and truthfully as we can, the foolish conventionalities of a large proportion of the middle classes of the present day, who believe that position is attained by climbing up a staircase of moneybags.' Delightfully illustrated.

Originally published 1847. · Size 13cm x 10.5cm

128 Pages Paperback, Illustrated. ISBN 0 946014 39 6 **£4**.00

Albert Smith was one of the greatest showmen of the 19th century. His entertainments were as popular a feature of the capital as Madame Tussaud's and the Tower of London. This book was one of a series of fictionalised accounts that were very popular with Victorian readers.

EVERYBODY'S BOOK OF EPITAPHS

Being For The Most Part What The Living Think Of The Dead

Here lies my wife, a sad slattern and shrew
If I said I regretted her, I should lie too!

A look at epitaphs for the famous to the poor — some amusing, some sad, some historic, some enlightening, all fascinating.

Here lies John Wherdle, Parish Beedle
Who was so very knowing
His wisdom's gone, and so is he,
Because he left off growing.

Originally published 1885. Size 13.5cm x 10.5cm

128 Pages Paperback. ISBN 0 946014 38 8 **£4**.50

A full list of our publications sent on request. All books post and packing free.
PRYOR PUBLICATIONS
75 Dargate Road, Yorkletts, Whitstable, Kent CT5 3AE.
Tel/Fax: (01227) 274655

BURROUGHES & WATTS.

UNDER THE PATRONAGE
OF HER MAJESTY THE QUEEN,
H.R.H. THE DUKE OF EDINBURGH,
THE KING OF THE BELGIANS, THE KING OF GREECE,
H.S.H. PRINCE SOLTYKOFF,
H.R.H. THE GRAND DUKE OF BADEN,
S.A. LE PRINCE HÉRITIER D'EGYPT,
H.H. PRINCE HASSAN,
AND SOLE CONTRACTORS TO
HER MAJESTY'S WAR DEPARTMENT & ADMIRALTY

FOR

BILLIARD TABLES.

The only Prize Medal awarded for Billiard Tables, 1851—1862.

SPECIAL NOTICE.—B. & W. beg to draw attention to the fact that their Tables are finished with special care, the wood of which they are built having been cut and dried for years, so as to ensure the preservation of *their proper level.* The *cushions* are made of *pure Para rubber,* and are stuffed on the most approved scientific principles, to ensure the ball being thrown off at its proper angle. The slates are rubbed down till they are brought to a water-level, and each Table is tested by one of the firm. The *ivory balls* (of which a stock of 20,000 can be seen at Soho) receive especial attention, and are selected with great care from the best Asiatic teeth.

200 *Tables,* in various designs, and every description of wood, on view; 500 in process of manufacture, from which customers may select. Timber for 2,000 in Stock.

Burroughes & Watts make a *Billiard Table,* 12 feet by 6 feet, mahogany, including Billiard Balls, Cues, Rests, Butts, Marking Board, Brush, Chalks, Cover, and Iron, *for 55 guineas.*

Steam Works:—DEAN STREET, HOLLEN STREET, & RICHMOND BUILDINGS.

Offices and Show Rooms:—
19, SOHO SQUARE, LONDON, W.; and 87, MARKET STREET, MANCHESTER.

THE
𝕭𝖎𝖑𝖑𝖎𝖆𝖗𝖉 𝕹𝖊𝖜𝖘,

*A Journal of Billiards and other
Sports and Pastimes.*

Published Weekly during the Six
Winter Months,

PRICE 1D.

And Monthly during the Six
Summer Months,

PRICE 2D.

THE MONTHLY NUMBERS CONTAIN A SPLENDID
COLOURED PORTRAIT.

---

*POST FREE ALL THE YEAR ROUND
FOR 4s. 6d.*

OFFICE:

18, CATHERINE ST., STRAND, W.C.

LAND AND WATER,

Under entirely New Management,

CONTAINS EVERY WEEK

NATURAL HISTORY, as practically applied to the study of Beasts, Birds, Fishes, Insects, and Plants; their habits and use to man.

SHOOTING.—News from Shooting Quarters; Notes, Queries, and Discussions on Game Preservation; Management of Dogs and Shows; Useful Inventions relating to Fire Arms,&c.

HUNTING.—Lists of Appointments direct from the kennels; Special Letters from the Hunting Field during the Season; Veterinary Notes, &c.

FISHERIES.—Latest Intelligence for Anglers; Commercial Products of Rivers; Deep-sea Fisheries; Oyster Cultivation; Correspondence on all questions relative to Fish Culture, especially Legislation.

YACHTING REPORTS of Matches; Yachting Intelligence from the various Stations; Articles on Yachting Subjects.

AQUATICS.
ATHLETICS.
CRICKET.
BILLIARDS. } Latest Reports from Universities, and a Critique on passing Important Events on the River, the Running Path, the Cricket Field, and Billiard Table.

PUBLIC SCHOOLS.—A Special Weekly Letter from each, noting their doings in and out of School.

ESTATE, FARM, TURF, GARDEN, YACHTING, CHESS, CROQUET, TRAVELLER, ARCHERY, THEATRES, LADIES' CORNER,

ALL ARE TREATED IN A PRACTICAL AND INSTRUCTIVE SUMMARY,

And any novelties in these Departments, if sent to the Office carriage paid, examined and reported upon.

PRICE SIXPENCE.

Free by Post, quarterly, 6s. 6d.; half-yearly, 13s.; yearly, £1 6s.
P.O.O. made payable to J. THORNELOE, on the Ludgate Circus Office.

ADVERTISEMENTS.

Sixty Words and under, 5s.; each additional Ten Words, 6d.

Special arrangements made for a Series.

OFFICE, 169, FLEET STREET, LONDON, E.C.